I0202008

Copyright © 2012 Shawna K. Lindsey

All rights reserved.

ISBN: 061560157X

ISBN-13: 978 - 0615601571

UNBOUND,

UNBLINDED,

AND REDEEMED:

MY JOURNEY FROM MORMONISM TO CHRISTIANITY

DEDICATION

To My Lord Jesus Christ

Who alone gives us His Amazing Grace

ACKNOWLEDGMENTS

To Larry Lindsey for challenging me with the truth and being a place of refuge when my world crumbled. To Lance, Rochelle, Jennifer, Damon, Micah, Justice, and Silas for bringing me into their family with support and love. To Pastor Ken Duggan, Pastor David McNabb, and all the staff at Dallas Bay Baptist Church for their enriching teachings of truth. To all the members of the Gatekeepers Sunday School class for their constant prayers and support. To Lacy Pauley and other Gatekeepers teachers for theirsolid biblical lessons. To the staff and faculty of CovingtonTheological Seminary, especially Dr. Hutchings and Karen Jenkinsfor their encouragement and support. To other friends and familyfor being there.

CONTENTS

All that is necessary for the triumph of evil is that good men do nothing.

Edmund Burke

CHAPTER ONE

WRAPPED UP TIGHT IN SILK CHAINS

My first exposure to Mormonism was in July of 1972 when I was nine years old. My dad had gotten a job as a microbiologist at Texas Tech University in Lubbock, Texas. My mom, my sister and I moved to Lubbock from Rossville, Georgia. My dad had spent the previous two years doing post-doctorate work at Stanford University in California. The same time we moved to Lubbock, a Mormon family moved in across the street from us. They had two daughters about the same age as me and my sister. We became friends with them. They started taking us to church with them sometimes, especially to children's activities during the week. We also spent time with them doing "family home evening" where they had scripture lessons and snacks.

My parents divorced three years after we moved to Lubbock. About a year later, my mom started dating a Mormon man whom she met through our Mormon neighbors. They were married two years later in 1977. My new step-dad wanted us to join the Mormon Church. We took a trip in our camper not long after they got married and we drove by many Mormon temples on the way to Canada. I did not think much about them at the time. They just seemed like pretty buildings to me. At the time I did not realize how much these temples would impact my life. My mom took the Mormon missionary discussions in 1978 and was baptized into the church. One year later in 1979 my sister and I took the missionary discussions and were baptized into the church. I was sixteen years old. I attended church for about six months and then stopped going.

I came to Rossville, Georgia to stay with my grandmother for a while in October of 1983, when I was twenty. While I was there my cousin's husband who was a new Christian witnessed to me, and I accepted Jesus Christ as my Savior. In my concern for my family, and in my desire to share with them the joy that I had received, I went back to Lubbock, Texas in January of 1984. Not understanding the truth about Mormon doctrine at the time and not knowing enough about the Bible, when I went back to Lubbock I began attending the Mormon Church again.

Two months later I met my former husband. We of course were encouraged to be married in a Mormon temple for "time and all eternity". In July we drove to Salt Lake City, Utah and were "sealed" in the Mormon temple. My former husband then started medical school in Lubbock and we spent the next eight years in Lubbock, going to school and raising our three children who were born in 1985, 1987, and 1989. We spent hours serving in callings in the Mormon Church over these years. We had made "sacred" covenants in the temple in Salt Lake City that we would obey all the laws of the church, and give everything we had (time, talent, money), and even our lives to the church or "allow our lives to be taken". These were oaths and covenants we made in the "House of the Lord" when we went through the temple in

1984. Our dedication to the church came from false beliefs we had that the Church was "the only true church on the earth today" and that it was teaching us what God wanted us to do, and how God wanted us to live; but in all actuality we were controlled by an unconscious fear of breaking the covenants that we had entered into. We knew that if we left the church and violated our covenants, we would not be together as a family for eternity, and we would be under the extreme and severe judgment of God. The Mormon Church claims the authority to grant salvation, exaltation, the gift of the Holy Ghost and many other blessings. They also claim the right to take all these things away too.

My former husband had moved to America from Montevideo, Uruguay in South America. He had been raised Catholic and had left his country in 1972. He had become a Mormon in 1982, about a year before we met. We both had been raised in troubled family situations. We believed that the Mormon Church would give us the family life that we had not had. We hoped that the standards the church taught would help us to avoid some of the tragic situations that we had experienced growing up.

Unfortunately, I had no idea how very far away the Mormon Church was from being a true Christian church. I was twenty when I got married and did not have a clue about what the true doctrines of the Bible were. I had no understanding about how anti-biblical Mormon doctrine was. I had no realization that the Mormon Church was a cult. From the time I was nine years old in 1972 and my sister and I started spending time in our neighbor's house, I associated many good emotions with the Mormon Church and the people. Nothing seemed to be dangerous or frightening in how I was treated by them. They seemed to me as a child as nice people who cared about me. There were no indications

3

that these people had any intentions that would be harmful to me.

We attended church as a family on a consistent basis from the time we were married. Our children went to children's primary classes and learned all about Mormonism from the time they were toddlers. The Mormon Church, because of its comprehensive laws and teachings, is its own culture. Most of our time was spent with other Mormons. Many of the Mormons we were around in Lubbock were professors and students at Texas Tech. Mormons put a lot of emphasis on education. There is no paid ministry in Mormonism, so the Church functions mostly on volunteer hours given by members. It is a lot different however than working in another Church. As a Mormon you are taught to believe that the Kingdom of God has been restored to the earth through Joseph Smith and any work you do in the Mormon Church or in your community is kingdom work. The Church administration is structured as a hierarchy, much like the Catholic Church. Each ward has a bishop who is a lay minister with no training, but is considered the father of the ward. You go to a particular Church building depending on where you live in the city. There are ward boundaries that are adhered to. You do not have a choice where you go to Church; it is determined only by where you live. All men in the Mormon Church bear the Melchizedek Priesthood. This is seen as the authority to act in the name of God on the earth. They see this authority as having come directly from Jesus Christ through the apostle Peter. Joseph Smith taught that Peter, James, and John actually returned to earth and gave him the "keys" for directing the Kingdom of God on earth through the Melchizedek Priesthood. All Mormon boys receive the Aaronic Priesthood when they turn twelve years old. They are expected to pass the sacrament each Sunday at church, as well as collect fast offerings from the members. All boys are also expected to progress through cub scouts and boy scouts.

Being inside the Mormon Church, my son recently mentioned, is like being in a "velvet prison." So much of the experience seems white, wholesome, and clean. People are encouraged to have very high standards in every area of their lives. They are expected to dress modestly, speak reverently, cherish their families, love their neighbors, do volunteer work, be good citizens, etc. They are also expected to faithfully attend all their Church meetings, "magnify" all their callings, do genealogy work, do temple work, get a good education, keep the Sabbath Day holy, live the Word of Wisdom (dietary laws), be good mothers and fathers, be active and responsible citizens, pray as individuals morning and night, pray as families daily, read Scriptures daily, serve a mission, pay tithing, etc. As a Mormon one is constantly encouraged to "be perfect as your Father in heaven is perfect". In order to continue to return to the temple to do temple work, one must have a personal worthiness interview by a Bishop and a Stake President (leader over several wards – next in hierarchy above a Bishop). You are asked many probing questions about your worthiness. You are expected to be worthy in every way before attending the temple.

Some of my early memories about Mormon activities at the ward building in Lubbock, Texas were of pioneer days in the summer. These events were celebrations with games and food and fellowship. I have good memories about taking part in these activities. Nothing about these things seemed "cultish". I remember feeling as a ten year old child that these people had happy, healthy lives. I always remember feeling safe and content at primary activities and other Church activities. I remember seeing the food storage that our neighbors had stored in their garage. I remember them always being very nice to us.

During the eight years we spent in Lubbock during my former husband's medical training, the church seemed like a good place for us to be. We enjoyed going to church together as a family. We met many nice people who seemed to love and support each other. It was almost as if we were being wrapped up tight in a cocoon. It was a consistent reality in our everyday lives. It gave us roles to play, and told us how to play them. It seemed to support our lives as a young family, and we were quite satisfied in the church during these years.

CHAPTER 2

IT IS ALL ABOUT THE KINGDOM

We moved to Nashville in 1992 and spent one year there. Our time in the Mormon ward in Franklin, Tennessee was different from our time in Lubbock. We did not get to know people quite as well, and it seemed like it was hard to fit in somehow. The following year we moved to Dayton, Ohio. My former husband had joined the Air Force and was sent to Wright-Patterson AFB. We moved into the boundaries of a small ward located in Fairborn, Ohio. Most of the members there were affiliated with the Air Force. It was the smallest ward in the "stake" (organization of several wards put together). People in this ward were sometimes given as many as three callings at one time. I was called to serve as a leader in the Young Women's organization soon after we arrived. There were some challenges with one of the young women, who was a daughter of a Stake President. The Bishop gave my former husband and me the task of dealing with her and her boyfriend. The Bishop was in some way trying to undermine the authority of the Stake President. We were left not knowing who to support. Most people are not aware how much being in the Mormon Church is like being in the military. You are expected to "sustain and support" your Priesthood leaders. Twice a year at General Conference (which is transmitted by Satellite to all Mormon buildings over the world) you are asked to openly vote and raise your right hand to sustain the Church leaders, beginning with the Prophet (President) of the Church, his two counselors, and the twelve apostles, the quorums of the seventy, and the presiding bishop and other leaders, including your local leaders. Over my years in the Church as a member of record from 1979 until 2008, I never saw one person vote against their leaders. They would verbally be given an opportunity to vote against someone, but because of the procedure being an "open ballot," this never happened. It was unspoken but true that you could not be a faithful Latter-day Saint, and not support your leaders. Everything in the Mormon Church is top-down. Everything is based upon Priesthood presiding authority. It is understood by all members that the Kingdom of God is on the earth, and the Mormon Church holds all the keys to operate God's Kingdom.

So it was very confusing for us in this small Ohio ward that the Bishop was undermining the authority of the Stake President. We agonized over who to support. It may seem trivial to people outside of the church, but this is a vital concept within the church. There is no room to get out of line. In the home it was seen that the husband "presided," using his Priesthood authority. Of course he was subject in some ways to the authority of the Bishop, as the father of the ward, and then to the Stake President who was the presiding High Priest over the stake. Each man in the Mormon Church, depending on whether he was an elder or a High Priest, functioned in a Priesthood Quorum in the ward. Through this they would see to the needs of members of the ward and function in a hierarchy, with an Elder's Quorum President or a High Priest Group leader over them. All adults in the Mormon Church were also responsible for being home and visiting teachers. You are assigned specific individuals or families to visit on a regular basis. This was for the purpose to teach them a lesson, or administer to any other needs they have. The church in many ways functions as a government over people's lives. There are distinct parameters in place that determine who you are, what you do, and what your roles are.

There is a threefold mission of the church which we were taught was critical to fulfill: 1. To spread the Gospel. 2. To redeem the dead. 3. To perfect the saints. Everything that was done in the church was to fulfill one of these three purposes. We were constantly encouraged to give away Book of Mormons. I believe one year in Ohio my former husband, as an Air Force Major, gave away about eight Books of Mormon to other Air Force doctors and nurses. This was part of what we thought God wanted us to do. Often in our meetings on Sunday, someone would be asked to stand up and speak about their experience giving away a Book of Mormon. We were expected to represent the church well everywhere we were, at work, in the community, with friends, etc. We knew at all times that when someone saw us, they were being sent a message about the kingdom, and we knew that we wanted everyone to become part of the kingdom, so we needed to be as perfect as possible at all times. We were encouraged continually by our leaders including the Bishop, High Council member, Stake President, or even the Prophet or Apostles to do temple work in order to offer salvation to our deceased ancestors. In order to do this, we needed to remain worthy to be able to continue to attend the temple.

The first temple I attended was the Salt Lake City, Utah temple in 1984 when we were married. Over the next twenty-two years many temples were built. I did temple work in temples in Idaho Falls, San Diego, Dallas, Chicago, Atlanta, Mesa Arizona, Nashville, Washington D.C., Denver, Los Angeles, and London England. Often we were encouraged to attend the temple at least once a month, if a temple was less than one day's drive away, and about once a week if there was a temple in the city where we lived. The small ward we moved into in Ohio was in the Chicago temple area. On a regular basis, this ward would rent a bus and take about thirty people to the Chicago temple. We would leave on Friday afternoon and drive about six hours to Chicago and stay overnight in a motel. Early on Saturday morning we would get up and go to the temple and start working around 8 A.M. Often the people of this small ward would feel compelled to do as many as seven temple sessions in a row, which would take all day long (each endowment or sealing session lasting about an hour and a half). Many times they would go without eating, or even taking a break. Afterwards, we would load up in the bus and drive back to the Dayton area, not arriving until late at night. Of course we would need to go to church the next day as part of the Sabbath activities. In this small ward I was asked to serve as Young Women's President. I was responsible for the Young Women's meetings, and any lessons they had on Sundays, also fireside meetings they had on Sunday nights. There were also other weekday meetings that had to be organized. There were meetings with both the Young Women and Young Men that needed to be held. Once a month there were ward correlation meetings in the Bishop's office for all the auxiliary leaders to coordinate their individual programs. In this small ward the Bishop often kept us in these meetings for four hours. He would call on individuals to "bear their testimony" of the church. Testimony meetings for the entire ward were held once a month on Sundays. These were called "fast and testimony" meetings. Everyone was expected to fast for at least two meals, and then donate the money saved in buying food during this time to the church to be used as fast offerings. At this meeting, the Bishop or one of his two counselors, would usually get up first and bear their testimonies. Then they would turn the time over to the members to follow suit one by one. There was usually a similar format to everyone's testimony. Everyone would almost always start with "I know the Church is true and that Joseph Smith was a true prophet". Very young children were often encouraged by their parents to get up and bear their testimonies. The words they spoke were whispered to them in their ears by their mothers or fathers. Often what would follow was an expression of gratitude for what God was doing in their lives, and how the Church and following its principles was blessing their lives. Sometimes people would break down and cry, but not always.

All three of our children were baptized in Ohio. Mormon children are expected to be taught the gospel by their parents, and be prepared for baptism at age eight (considered the age of accountability). They are baptized by their fathers or another man as long as he holds the Melchizedek Priesthood, and has the authority to perform this ordinance. A Priest in the Aaronic Priesthood actually is considered to have the authority to baptize (this would be boys who have turned 16). After being baptized, they are sat in a chair and surrounded by men who hold the Melchizedek Priesthood, have hands placed on their head and are given the gift of the Holy Ghost. They are also "voted into fellowship" by all the ward members on the following Sunday. Their name is presented by the Bishop or his

11

counselors, and the members are asked to raise their right hand to accept them into the Church in full fellowship, and into the records of the Church. Records are an enormous part of the Mormon Church, and every ordinance is recorded by the Ward Clerk or Ward Secretary (both Priesthood callings). The member is then presented with a formal certificate of the ordinance. Also, when children are born to church members, they are expected to be brought before the ward sometime during their first couple of months, and be given "a name and a blessing". The baby is carried by the father to the front of the sanctuary, held by the father, and surrounded by Melchizedek Priesthood holders. They then bow their heads and the father announces that this child will be known throughout his life, and on the records of the Church as _____. Then the father pronounces a blessing on the child, which will usually, includes blessings of health, wisdom, and a mission and temple wedding in the future. This is something that my former husband did with all three of our children.

The small ward we attended in Ohio functioned like a family. Every Labor Day, Memorial Day, and Columbus Day we would have ward picnics in a state park near Enon, Ohio. These would be all day gatherings with hikes, football games, and lots of food. We also had ward activities, and for about a year I was the ward activity director and organized Christmas parties and other events for the ward. Everything in the Mormon Church is about families. Inside the Church families are encouraged to love and serve each other. There are continual lessons about how to be good parents, and how to be obedient children. Women attend Relief Society meetings on Sunday mornings, while the men attend Priesthood meetings. Mormons meet for three hours for church each Sunday, in which one hour is for Priesthood and Relief Society meetings. One hour is for Sunday school, and the other hour is for Sacrament meeting for the entire ward. There are no preachers, so in sacrament meeting there is a format that is usually followed. The Bishop or his counselor preside, and are in charge of the meeting. There is an opening song and opening prayer given by a man or woman who is asked to do so. Then the youngest priesthood holders, the deacons, pass the sacrament (bread and water), after the older priesthood holders, the priests in the Aaronic priesthood bless the sacrament. The priest (16 or 17 yr old boy) pronounces the same blessing "word for word" over the bread, and then the water and the younger boys pass these to members of the congregation. Before this, any ward business is taken care of; which includes people being called, or released from callings and the entire ward voting on each one. After the sacrament is passed there is usually a teenager who gives a 5-10 minute talk, a woman who gives a 10 minute talk, and finally a man who gives a 15 minute talk about whatever subject the Bishop has assigned to them. Usually as a family, you are asked to speak about once a year on average. There are usually choir songs performed, and maybe a song from the Hymnbook that is sung in between the talks.

There are many church requirements that need to be met by children, such as memorization of the church's articles of faith as well as other goals that include self-discipline and service. It is the same for young men and women. There are awards presented during sacrament meetings for each achievement, which are usually presented by the Bishop in front of the entire ward. The young men's program is Boy Scouts. Mormon boys are encouraged to become Eagle Scouts at least by age 16 if possible. Both of my sons became eagle scouts at about this age. There are always recognitions in the church for scouting achievements. Young women are mostly encouraged to put their focus on going to the temple someday to be sealed for time and eternity, homemaking skills, etc. They are encouraged to develop divine attributes, and during their meetings each Sunday, they stand and repeat the same words about who they are and what God expects them to be and how they do it. Some of the lines I remember are … "We are daughters of our heavenly father, who loves us and we love him, we will stand as witnesses of God, at all times and in all things and in all places… we believe in following the young women values, which are faith, divine nature, individual worth, knowledge, choice and accountability, good works, and integrity… we believe as we come to accept and act upon these values, we will be prepared to enter the temple, make and keep sacred covenants, strengthen home and family…" It went something like this at least. This was repeated by all the girls every Sunday, at the first of the meetings as they stood and said these things by memory.

CHAPTER 3

THE VELVET PRISON OF THE KINGDOM OF JOSEPH SMITH

The reality of all these things is that a "velvet prison" is still a prison, and "silk" chains are still chains. Inside, it appears to be white and wholesome, but in the same way that people living in Germany before World War II thought that Hitler had brought them hope as he placed them under false worship and a "sense" of order, being a part of the Mormon Kingdom of God is the same. It is wholly and completely the program of man being enabled to exalt himself, and become like God. Inside this velvet prison, there is such an overpowering false sense of security, that from deep inside of it, it is completely unthinkable to ever consider turning away from it. So much of it "seems" right, that the thought of it ever being truly wrong, never crosses one's mind. The fact that in any Mormon Church building anywhere in the world on the same Sunday, everyone is taught the same Sunday School, Relief Society, or Priesthood lesson is troubling. There is within the Mormon church, a level of mind control used which technologically is probably not being used in the same way as efficiently by any other church or government in the world. They keep people very much on the same page at the same time, and mobilize people to act in unison during disasters, as well as during elections. In every ward I was in, there was always a call chain that was put into place for emergencies. There were often letters that would be read from the pulpit by a Bishop or his counselor on Sundays, which would often involve "semi" political topics. Perfect obedience to the leaders is what is expected from the members.

Turning from the "soft chains and bars" of Mormonism to some of the underlying realities that exist among Mormons is necessary to be able to understand the church. Much is hidden from the world. Only from the inside can one see the cracks in what is presented to the outside world to be so "perfect." In all reality, over my thirty-five years of involvement with the Mormon Church, I saw many things that caused much concern. I served in the Mormon Women's organization (Relief Society) in various leadership capacities for about ten years. Especially during these years, I was made aware of abuse of various forms. Many women shared with me their own experiences of having been sexually abused by fathers, or other male relatives. Others were being hit by their husbands or sons. There were many who were constantly demeaned and ridiculed by their husbands. I would say that over sixty-five percent of the Mormon women I knew over all my years in the church were taking medication for depression or bipolar disorder. Often it seemed that women would have emotional or nervous breakdowns when they reached the age of forty. Many women had very large families which placed enormous burdens on them, which oftentimes they were unable to deal with. Women were continually expected to be perfect, and perform to their full capacity as wives and mothers, as well as do a myriad of other activities also. I once worked with a woman who had eleven children (six still at home at the time), who was serving as Relief Society President, PTA president at her children's elementary school, and also working part time at the University teaching business (she had a Master's degree in business). She also would regularly make things at home around Christmas which she would sell to make extra money for the family. She was a hard working and dedicated Mormon woman to say the least.

Another concern about the abusive situations that I saw, was the fact that the Bishops and Stake Presidents had no training in ministry or counseling whatsoever. What they did was volunteer their time to serve as church leaders, but continue to work at full-time jobs every day. They would follow church guidelines for discipline as well as counseling with people. I witnessed many times a lack of capacity on their part to obtain any real help for people who were in desperate situations in their personal lives. The Mormon Church has a social services division which includes counselors, but most people are not encouraged to use them. Any problems are often seen as the fault of the member in not being "faithful" enough to the church, and to its programs. Many people were often encouraged to just pray and read their scriptures more (Mormon scriptures being the Bible, the Book of Mormon, the Doctrine and Covenants, and the Pearl of Great Price). Several times there were unexpected suicides which occurred among church members. Within the church you cannot be broken. This is in complete opposition to what the Church teaches. You are seen as failing the church if you become broken. There were never times of prayer requests in any church meetings. Intercessory prayer is not really a part of Mormonism. There was only a place that you could secretly put a person's name in a container in the temples so that the temple patrons could pray for these people during part of the endowment ritual (in a prayer circle), even though these temple patrons are not aware of any specific concerns or names, it all being kept secret.

As the Mormon Church is promoting the development of a "perfect person" or "perfect race" (for people to become gods), similar to what Hitler did, there is no room for misfits. I once knew a handicapped man who was in a wheelchair who was told that he could no longer serve in the temple because he was "too old," as well as not married. Women who could not have children suffered tremendously in Mormonism. A Mormon woman's value is largely based upon her ability to "bring spirits to the earth." and when she was unable to do this, ultimately she was prevented from truly being able to assist God in procreation. Children who were overweight or handicapped were often not viewed as being as valuable as others, as their ability to show forth perfection was obviously lacking.

The pressure on Mormon boys to serve a two year mission is one that people outside of the church cannot understand. From a time a little boy is speaking and walking he is taught songs like "I hope they call me on a mission," which continually send the message that to please God you must serve a "valiant" mission. There is that spoken and unspoken message sent year after year that one day that day would arrive when the Prophet will call you to serve your mission, and you will be able to sacrifice two years, and share the fullness of the gospel with others. This is held as such an opportunity and honor to fulfill, that when a young man does not go on a mission, or if he returns early from his mission, he is seen by his family and the ward, as a disappointment and failure. I have seen boys over the years suffer humiliation and ostracism because they did not go on a mission, or returned early for various reasons. Girls may go on a mission when they turn twenty-one, but this usually is somewhat of a sign that they were not privileged to be chosen by a Priesthood holder and married in the temple before this time. I saw many girls be sent to BYU University to find a husband, not really ever expected to complete their own education. It was often expected of girls, after they met their future spouses at BYU or other colleges, to quit school and support their husband after they got married, while the husband finished his education. If a Mormon girl is not married to a returned missionary by the time she is 22 or 23, her family usually become very concerned about her future in the church.

Another thing Mormon youth are expected to do is to attend early morning seminary classes when they start to high school. These are usually held at about 6:30 A.M. every weekday morning for about an hour before school. Regular attendance at seminary classes is strongly encouraged by the Bishop and other youth leaders. My sons and daughter attended "release time" seminary classes in an LDS seminary building across the street from their high school. The Mormon Church actually has support from public school systems which allows these students to leave campus one hour a day to attend these classes. There was no separation of church and state issues involved with this. This is often how Mormon Church seminaries are set up in places where there are large numbers of LDS children. There is status in the Mormon Church from sending your child to BYU. This is encouraged, and Mormons who do so are held in high esteem among other Mormons. It is very difficult, however, to be accepted into BYU, as there are so many Mormon young adults wanting to go there.

19

Being a Mormon is something one does 24 hours a day, seven days a week, wherever you are and with whomever you are around. Over the years I spent as a Mormon, I made various friends who were Christians. I thought that as a Mormon, I was a Christian. I did not understand and could not see the vast difference in what they believed and in what I believed. I was taught that other Christians, who were not Mormons, did not have the "fullness" of the gospel; they only had part of it. They were not as blessed as I was, because they did not really know who they were. They did not know that they were children of God from the time they were born. They did not know that they had lived with their heavenly father and mother in pre-existence as a spirit child of theirs, and that they had been faithful there, and had "chosen" to come to earth because in the grand council in heaven they chose Jesus' plan of salvation (Jesus being our first born spirit brother) over Lucifer's plan of salvation (Lucifer being another spirit brother). I was taught that Jesus gave us free agency in his plan, but Lucifer's plan was rejected because he took away man's free agency. Other Christians did not know the sacred fact that God had been a man, and that he had "progressed" to become a god, and that they too could become gods if they followed the "fullness" of the gospel and its teachings. They did not know that if they joined the church, they could hold the priesthood if they were men and "bless" their families with authority directly from God. The other Christians I knew seemed to accept me as a Christian, and together with them I did work in the community, in College, and in politics, as we often had the same moral and ethical agendas. It was very rewarding to know that they trusted me to join with them and fight for similar things such as family values, voter integrity, drug laws, abortion, and community safety. I knew any time I spent in community service, and any involvement in the political process would

20

help me share in some way the blessings of the Kingdom of God. We were often encouraged to let people know we were Christians, and we wanted to be accepted as such.

The very sad reality however was that I was not in a Christian Church, and what I believed was completely different from Christians I knew. They, however, were mostly unaware of what I really believed, and not one of them ever tried to challenge what I believed, until I met my husband almost three and a half years ago. I met a Christian friend in 1991 while I was working on my Bachelor's degree at Texas Tech. Her husband was a pilot in the Air Force. She even came and took part in a Relief Society talent show with me. She never really understood what I believed; she just knew we seemed to have similar standards. For seven years in New Mexico we lived across the street from a couple who attended a large Baptist Church. We got to know them very well and I helped her in Neighborhood/political/zoning issues with the city. She never really knew that what I believed was so different from what she believed. I also worked with a Christian State Senator in New Mexico, and she put a lot of trust in me and seemed to accept that our beliefs were similar. She did not actually have any idea what I believed, and especially she did not realize how my involvement in the Mormon Church was such an enormous part of my life. What I did in politics and the community was inseparable with what I did in the church. It is hard to explain, but Mormons see their influence in the community and in the political realm as an extension of church work. It is helping to bring forth the Kingdom of God. I believed in the Constitution, and had become very familiar with it after attending Law School in Columbus, Ohio. I felt that the Constitution was an inspired document, as I had been taught as a Mormon. What other people around me though did not realize, is that I knew that the Constitution was only temporary, that someday the Kingdom of God – the Mormon Church, would spread over the entire earth and then the "perfect" government would be in place, ruled only by the Priesthood of God. This was such an integral part of what I believed, the time I spent assisting the New Mexico State Senator, representing the Republican party in the ballot recount in 2000, serving on the Rules Committee of the State Republican Party, as well as working with voter integrity issues was all part of my "Kingdom" work. When I moved to the Chattanooga area in 2006, the first job I took was as a field marshal in the Bob Corker United States Senate campaign. It was thrilling for me to see how BYU Idaho sent us about thirty students to help during the last few days of the campaign in making thousands of phone calls. Bob Corker's success was partially attributed to the hours of free work these Mormon students gave to his campaign. I was proud of them, especially the way that they "joyfully" gave of their time to the political process. Many other volunteers in the campaign, including Bob Corker's family were quite taken by their generosity and kindness. They celebrated their way throughout his victory, and in the end did a wonderful job for the Mormon Church in promoting the patriotic and hard-working image of the LDS Church members. Every time I did any political or community work I let people know I was a Mormon. I knew that by promoting the Church through my action and attitudes, I was fulfilling at least a part of the threefold mandate of the Church to spread the gospel.

Inside a velvet prison, even though one may be held by "silk" chains, when you look a little closer you see the cold, hard walls that are only velvet covered. Most of what I have already written is only a glimpse of the outer layer of the prison, one that is often acceptable by the outside world and how the church is thought of by believing Mormons. The next inner layer of brokenness, I mentioned before. The saddest reality is that in the softness of this "prison," one is lulled into a false security, believing that his or her salvation is secure. The saddest cases in Mormonism, ultimately, are the ones that "thrive" for generations there. There are many Mormon families, especially out west, who pride themselves on their Mormon pioneer ancestry. It is a mark of distinction for a Mormon to have descended from pioneer stock. Often in sacrament meetings one will get up and read from their pioneer ancestor's journals, about the sacrifices that they made during the early days of the Church. There is an unspoken level of respect that goes along with ancestry, and often this seems to influence specific "high" church positions that people are called to. Because I and my former husband had none of these, there were times when we did not feel as worthy as those who had been privileged to have pioneer ancestry. Mormonism, being not just a church, but a culture, creates families that have for generation after generation, done what they have done, just because of tradition. Tradition is an enormous part of Mormonism, especially the closer one gets to Utah.

CHAPTER 4

MY FREEDOM AS A DAUGHTER OF PERDITION

The most horrible thing a Mormon is ever told about, which is so bad it is almost never spoken of is an "apostate". Over my many years as a Mormon, I had heard about apostates, but I had never known one. I knew there were inactive Mormons, like my mother had been for many years, who were just choosing not to participate in the church, for only a season hopefully. Apostates though, were nearly unmentionable. The sad fact being, that if a temple going Mormon even associates with an apostate, they are considered unworthy of returning to the temple. To a believing Mormon what this does is jeopardize his or her family being together for eternity. It also puts at risk his or her eternal temple marriage, as well as personal exaltation. There are thousands of inactive Mormons. Recently I spoke to a friend of mine who joined the Mormon Church through my influence back in 1985. She only remained active for a very short time, but she continued to have visitors from the

Mormon Church come to her house over the next 28 years. Her name continued to be on the records of the Church, and she was seen as an "inactive" member, who would hopefully come back someday. She never did, however, and I believe has since gone through the somewhat rigorous process of having her name removed from the Mormon Church records. There is a world of difference between an inactive Mormon and an apostate. An apostate is seen as an enemy of the Church. In all reality most apostates are former Mormons who have become Christians, and feel compelled by God to reach out and help the Mormon people. Often in their reaching out, however, it is perceived by a Mormon as attacking their beliefs. Trying to describe how horrible an apostate is to a Mormon is difficult. I would say that it is similar to being the most hated and despised kind of person you can imagine, maybe like a child molester/murderer is seen by many in our society. Being an apostate carries a stigma in Mormon culture that is profound to say the least.

So, in my own journey, two years ago on April 12th, Easter Sunday, I became an apostate. At the same time that I became an apostate to my family and former Mormon friends, I became an un-blinded Christian to others. It took a lot to open my eyes. Because I had become a born-again believer way back in 1983, to say that I grieved God's Spirit in a tremendous way for many years is a complete understatement. God blessed me while I was a Mormon in making me very uncomfortable.

After moving to Ohio in 1993, I became somewhat disillusioned with the Church. I think it began when my former husband's parents came to America in 1990 and moved in with us. At the time, I was serving as a counselor in the Relief Society Presidency. I also was trying to finish my Bachelor's degree, and take care of three small children.

26

When my husband's parents moved in, I realized that I could not see to their needs and the needs of my children and continue to function in my church calling. I asked to be released, and was chastised for doing so by a Mormon lady, and told that no one asks to be released from a calling, but one needs to wait for God to let the Bishop know you need to be released. I felt like I had done the right thing though. After moving to Ohio and being asked to serve in the Young Women's program as counselor and then as President, I was overwhelmed with the number of meetings that were required, and with the extreme length of some of these meetings. Our bishop would have personal priesthood meetings with me once a month when I was Young Women's President that lasted for four hours at a time. It all seemed very fanatical to me. The Church during these years in Ohio became a burden to us as a family.

There were also strange occurrences that seemed very unusual. Our Bishop there spoke about hearing Jesus walk through the halls of the ward building, and also through his home. There seemed to be a fascination among some of the members with Mormon Church history, as we were living not too far from Kirtland, Ohio where some strange events in Church history had taken place. The Bishop asked me to have a chair in our home that Jesus could come and sit in. After five years in Ohio we were quite confused about the Church. We also suffered a major car accident in 1995, which resulted in our seven year old son requiring neurosurgery for a skull fracture. We were all injured in the accident, but miraculously no one died. I had become totally confused at this time about my personal faith in Christ and the church. They seemed somehow to be at odds, but in my blindness I could not determine how. I started Law School in 1995, and spent much time involved in pursuit of my law degree for the next three and a half years. We continued to attend Church, but a lot of my focus had to be on school and my children. We moved to Albuquerque, New Mexico in 1998. Shortly after arriving there my father committed suicide several weeks after he turned 60 years old. This event seemed to taint my acceptance into Relief Society in the ward we moved into in Albuquerque. Probably the fact that I was finishing Law School at University of New Mexico Law School also seemed strange to other Mormon women I met. This was definitely not a typical or traditional thing for a Mormon woman to be doing. We kept going to Church though over the next seven years that we lived in Albuquerque. It seemed like the Church over these years became more and more just something that we could not live up to. It became tedious and exhausting. We were never good enough for it. We could never do enough to get it right. We never felt like we fit in. Especially in Albuquerque, where many Mormons had moved there from Utah, there was a sense that those who were not from Utah were not as good as other members. It was all quite frustrating to us as a family. I believe that mostly through these years that it was only the covenants we had made in the temple that kept us faithful in attending Church, mostly out of a fear that to "fail the church" would be to fail God.

In my heart from about 1994 on, I was so confused about what I believed about God and who He was, that my prayers became "thy will be done, not mine". For the next 14 years this was mostly the case, as I had no idea what was really wrong in what we were doing, or not doing. I knew that personally we were becoming more and more worn out and exhausted as individuals, and as a family. The pressure from the teachings of the church to be perfect, and live all the laws of the restored gospel, and continue to serve and sacrifice for God was depleting us completely. Our faithfulness to the

Mormon Church almost did us in. There was just no place for us to take our weariness into our Mormon faith. The Mormon god was continually requiring us to do all that we could do, before he would be ready to show us any mercy, and over time trying to do all that we could do was only breaking us down. Between the years 2000-2005 we struggled along, and eventually we came apart. My oldest son put his papers in to serve a mission in October of 2004, but he was rejected and told he was too overweight to serve a mission, even though his physician had given him a good report and said that he was healthy enough to go on a mission. Our mental, emotional, spiritual, and physical exhaustion finally ended up in our divorce in 2006. I moved to Chattanooga that year to live close to my mother and sister. I continued to attend the Mormon Church there, but was totally confused about everything.

In April of 2008 I met the man God sent into my life, who is now my husband. He was a Baptist, and had been a Christian for about 32 years. He was an answer to so many of my prayers in so many ways. Thankfully, we both felt that God had brought us together. He challenged me, not long after we were married, to put down the Book of Mormon, and read the New Testament. I started doing this around July of 2008. God began doing an amazing work in my heart and mind. God used this time to work on me intensely. My family turned away from me during this time, and was not speaking to me. My husband and I would have many long and sometimes heated discussions about the Bible, and what I believed. I cannot explain how much emotional pain I was in during these months. I was so confused, because of how my family was rejecting me, and about what I believed, that I will admit much of the time I did not even want to live. God had me just where He wanted me however, and I just wanted to run away. I did not though. God somehow kept letting me know that I could trust Him. I was terrified, and did not even realize that I was terrified about turning against the covenants I had made in the Mormon temple. I had stopped wearing the garments that all temple-going Mormons are required to wear night and day to protect them against "the power of the destroyer". This concerned me. But what concerned me more was that my husband kept telling me that Joseph Smith was a false prophet, etc. Each time he said this it was like having a knife stabbed deep into my heart. What I did not realize is that I had actually been brainwashed to "worship" Joseph Smith. One point I need to make is that there is no such thing as "praise" music in the Mormon Church. The only song I remember that mentioned praise was one which said "Praise to the man who communed with Jehovah, Jesus anointed that prophet and seer...," speaking of Joseph Smith. I also remember as a Mormon standing and singing "We Thank Thee O God for a Prophet," when the current prophet would enter a general conference meeting. This was the only praise that I was aware of. I had no idea how the God of the Bible was the awesome God of the Universe with His innumerable immutable characteristics and immensity. The god of Mormonism had once been a man and had become a god. In reality, this Mormon god was so small. He was also very demanding and exacting, and expected perfection in everything I did. I was terrified even to consider the possibility that Joseph Smith was a false prophet, and that the Mormon Church was not true. I could not even began to number the times that I had heard person after person over the past 36 years "testify" to the fact that Joseph Smith was a prophet of God. Hearing this time after time after time had placed Joseph Smith into a very sacred place inside my heart and mind. Having this challenged was physically and emotionally wrenching. However, my husband

and his passionate zeal for the truth, continued to challenge what I believed. At one point I became so frustrated that I took a set of Mormon Scriptures I had that included the Book of Mormon, the Doctrine and Covenants, The Pearl of Great Price, and the Bible and I ripped it apart and threw it in the trash. I was so exasperated. Slowly however, by reading the New Testament, and with the help of my husband explaining many basic doctrinal concepts, I began to see a different God emerge. It made it easier to begin to rest a little bit in the hope that I was headed in the right direction, even though so many things were still so confusing.

I had started attending Dallas Bay Baptist Church with him in April of 2008. It is hard to explain the experience of transitioning from attending a Mormon Church for so many years to an evangelical Baptist Church with praise music and preaching. The first time I attended the temple in 1984, and for the six years following, the temple ceremony called the "endowment," (where a film is shown which relates a perverted version of Genesis and the creation of the earth and the creation of Adam and Eve) also contained the character of Satan. Satan would enter onto the screen identifying himself at one point as a preacher. He was practicing "priestcraft" or preaching for money, which is warned about in the Book of Mormon (the Mormon Church having no paid ministry). Time after time the image of Satan identifying himself as a preacher had placed preachers into my subconscious as people to be wary and afraid of. So week after week, after I first started attending Dallas Bay, I would fight off tremendous feelings of panic and fear sitting in the congregation and listening to Pastor Ken preach his message. I would carefully listen though to what he was saying, kind of like I was peeking out from behind a big rock and see if I needed to literally run away from what I was hearing. I never

31

heard anything though that caused me much alarm. It was mostly my subconscious mind screaming that I was somehow in a danger zone. I would sit through these meetings often seized with fear, because it felt like I was suspended in mid-air, as if I needed to see where the walls or lines were drawn. It felt so free and open, much of it being terrifying to me on the one hand, but also very refreshing and liberating on the other. This was a strange time when I look back on it, because much of what I was feeling I did not share with anyone. I did not understand why I was feeling this way. I just knew that my life seemed to be taking a drastic turn.

We took a trip to Pennsylvania during late fall of 2008, and we drove into downtown Philadelphia one night. We walked by a large Masonic temple in Philadelphia, and my husband said he would like to know more about the Masons. When we returned home I found a used book about Masons, and he started reading some of it. I read some of it, and something struck me as strange. Much of what is done in the Masonic temple ceremony was very similar to what I had taken part in inside Mormon temples. This was the one thing that really made me begin to doubt the temple.

It was not long after this, after almost a year of not attending a Mormon Church, attending a Baptist Church, reading the New Testament for hours and hours, and not reading the Book of Mormon that I finally had enough courage, and was so fatigued too, that one Saturday night I prayed and asked God to let me know if the Book of Mormon and the Mormon Church were not true. The next day (Easter Sunday) April 12th 2009 it happened in an instant. God opened my eyes by the power of His Holy Spirit, and I saw clearly for the first time. I describe it as everything that was white became black, and everything that was black became white. It was the most profound day of my life, next to the day that I had asked Jesus to be my Savior way back in 1983. I saw all at once that I had been deceived. I saw that the Mormon Church was a cult, and that I had raised my children in a cult. I saw that I had been completely wrong about everything that I had believed and about so many things that I had done, because of how I believed. I say that it was the best day, and the worst day of my life.

I felt so betrayed. In my anger that day I told my husband that I would never walk through the doors of another church. I felt so used and violated. The next day or so I actually took a .357 handgun I owned, bought an old pair of cowboy boots at a Goodwill store, imagined they had belonged to Joseph Smith and "filled them full of holes". It made me feel a little better, but not really. The impact of my now being able to see completely overwhelmed me with a huge range of emotions. I knew that I loved God, but I saw how very horrible my actions had been. I did not know what to do. For the next several months I was overcome with guilt for what I had done in believing false doctrine, leading my children astray (even if unknowingly), as well as others in my family, and wanting desperately to be able to share the truth with the people I loved. They however would have none of it, and so I had to turn my anxiety over them to the Lord, or it would have destroyed me.

My sister, in her ignorance and blindness around this time convinced my daughter to move to Utah and go to BYU. Not long after I was un-blinded, my husband and I flew to Salt Lake City to attend a Christian conference called Compassionate Boldness, which was about reaching out to Mormons. It was a blessing for me to be around other former Mormons who had become Christians. We also visited my daughter and niece when we were out there. It was very sad though to see the things that happened to Mormons who

33

came out of the Church. Often their families would disown them, and not speak to them for years. They would also lose jobs, as well as marriages over leaving the Church.

After my eyes were opened, slowly I came to understand the God of the Bible more and more. My husband had taken several seminary classes before I met him, and several months after we were married I encouraged him to start taking classes again. I wanted to take some classes with him. I signed up late in 2008 to take seminary classes with him at Covington Theological Seminary, and I began a pursuit of a doctorate in Theology, actually several months before I was un-blinded.

The first class that we took together at the seminary was on the Apostle Paul which was taught by George Johnson. When we began attending this class in January of 2008, I would sit in class, once again overwhelmed with feelings of terror, because not only was I listening to a preacher, I was now actually an enrolled student in a seminary class. I knew that God was about to kill me at anytime. Week after week, I sat in class very uncomfortable and confused, but slowly learning more about Paul, whom I knew so very little about (His New Testament writings are not focused on much in the Mormon Church). His teachings on salvation by grace and grace alone were what I needed to learn and understand.

One week George actually made a comment about Joseph Smith being demon-possessed, and my husband thought that I might actually get up and leave. I did not though as I had become somewhat accustomed to Joseph Smith being spoken of in this way by my husband. Once again God kept letting me know that I just needed to relax, trust, and not run away.

What had actually been happening for about nine months before I was un-blinded was that I was being "deprogrammed" though I did not realize it. We live somewhat isolated out in the beautiful Tennessee hills near the Tennessee River, and this served a vital purpose during this time. I needed hour upon hour of God's Word to break through the misconceptions and lies that I had been indoctrinated with over many years. After I could see clearly, I also became extremely interested in the truth about Mormonism. I bought many books and spent hours doing research on the internet about this. I had met a lady named Sandra Tanner at the Compassionate Boldness Conference in Utah in April of 2009. Her and her husband had started a ministry in the 1960's reaching out to Mormons. They were probably the most well-known and well-hated Mormon apostates for many years, actually having a bookstore on Temple Square close to the Salt Lake Temple. Her website (utlm.org) was a wonderful resource for me in discovering the true history of the Mormon Church. There is also a website for ex-Mormons (exmormon.org) where many ex-Mormons express in writing what they are going through, and what they went through in the Mormon Church. I spent hours on this website reading what so many other former Mormons were experiencing. I could relate to so much of what was written on this website.

In the months to come, my husband and I would complete over 20 seminary classes together. The benefit to me to be able to learn so much about Christian biblical doctrine has been tremendous. As my false foundation of Mormonism came crumbling so painfully down in April of 2009, God's firm foundation found in His Word alone – the Bible - became vital to me. I do not believe that I would be alive today if it had not been for the love of my husband, and the amazing grace of my Savior aiding me hour after painful hour in passing from such darkness into such light so quickly. So many things I did not understand. My husband's faith has been like a rock to me, and our continual Bible study and prayer has been worth so much. I have spent an incalculable number of hours also over the past three years listening to Moody radio and various preachers. This has been so wonderful in nourishing me with more understanding of God's Word.

I also began writing on an almost daily basis about two weeks before my eyes were opened. I wrote for almost a year about what I was experiencing as I was emerging from the darkness and chains that had had me bound. I would begin each day by reading the Psalms, and then pray and allow God to guide me in what I wrote. I had so much to say about what I was going through. I had truly entered a new culture, with a new language and new ways of doing everything. Writing helped me to express so much that I needed to express about my experience.

I had many nightmares for months. I also had strong physical and emotional reactions to different words such as "covenant", "temple", and "sacrament". After I realized how incompatible and divergent Mormon doctrine was from biblical doctrine, I was haunted by so many things about Mormonism. I could clearly see the "warped" and "anti-Christ" nature of so much of Mormonism. I realized that the simple biblical doctrines, such as the fall, had been completely perverted by Joseph Smith. I was taught as a Mormon that man fell "upward," the fall being a good thing allowing man to bear children. I had been taught that polygamy was a divine institution from God. I was taught that a covenant was something that I made with God, and God would kill me if I broke it. I was taught that the Bible was not

36

inerrant, but had been translated incorrectly. I was taught that the Priesthood of the Mormon Church was how God chose to operate His authority on the earth today. I was taught that prophecy was something that was continually coming from the prophet of the Mormon Church, and that what he said was the same as Scripture. I had been taught that God had once been a man, and had elevated himself to become God, and that I needed to do the same thing. I had been taught that laws were necessary for salvation and exaltation, and that the self-exaltation of man to godhood was actually a good thing.

In all reality, I had carried a King James version of the Bible as part of my Mormon Scriptures for almost thirty years, but I had no idea what the Bible really said, or what its' main message was. I believed as a Mormon I was from the tribe of Ephraim, and was part of the twelve tribes of Israel. I had been given a patriarchal blessing when I was twenty-one by a Mormon patriarch, who was also an attorney and a Law School professor. He told me, as he laid his hands on my head, that the restored gospel had come to me as a familiar spirit, and that I was from the tribe of Ephraim, and that I would be blessed with various blessings during my life based on my faithfulness to the restored gospel. I was taught that Indians were actually of Jewish ancestry, and that the Book of Mormon was the "most correct book" on the earth today.

In my blindness, I could in no way understand the Bible the way I needed to. I know now however, that studying the New Testament for hours and hours for almost a year was how God worked in removing my blindness. It is the Word of God that is sharper than a two-edged sword which continually cut me to the center. It cut out false doctrine from my heart and mind on a daily basis. It was not a pleasant experience, but it was necessary. Slowly, my husband continually emphasizing for me certain true doctrines of the Bible, and my own bible study, became less painful and more rewarding.

During this time I felt such an overwhelming desire to be able to share what I had found out about the Mormon Church with the rest of the Mormons in my family, but it did not happen like I would have wanted it to. This is something that I have given over to God time and time again, and He is doing a work in their lives, although at this time there has been no significant contact between me and my sister and her family for the past three years. My husband and I have not been included in any family holidays or birthdays for three years now. I have somewhat adjusted to it, but it has caused a lot of pain at times, especially around Thanksgiving and Christmas. This is typical though of so many other Mormons that leave the Church.

It is amazing that an organization claiming to be all about the family can be so anti-family on the outside. If someone comes out of the Mormon Church, and renounces it as false, he or she often spend years separated from family members who are still in the Church. It destroys family relationships. It places its false doctrine and its interests above family relationships, and uses the sanctity of these relationships and the way God created us to live in families as weapons to keep people under its control. It is devastatingly demonic in the way it does this.

I have referred to the Mormon Church many times after realizing the truth about it as a "political organization" rather than a Church. This is how it functions. It only has the cover of being a church, but in all actuality is a multi-national, multi-billion dollar corporate organization, with tax-free status, which uses religion and family to enslave people to it.

Many Mormons who live far away from Utah have no idea what is actually being taught at BYU, or how missionaries are being trained or what they are being taught. Many other religious ideas are being incorporated into the curriculum at BYU. My daughter has shared with me recently, that in her six classes in Psychology, three of her textbooks teach evolution. One professor of hers has been teaching meditation and Buddhism, as well as a lot of other philosophical concepts. Mormon missionaries are also taught that Mohammed was a peace loving man, and that there is truth in all other religions.

Often Mormonism and Islam are seen as being similar, and in many ways they are. During the first trip we took to Salt Lake City in April 2009, one of my daughter's roommates had a good friend who was attending BYU who was a Muslim. This friend of my daughter's compared her friend wearing her hijab, as similar to how the Mormons wear garments. She felt very comfortable among the Muslims, and actually went and stayed with her friend's Muslim family in Israel for three weeks that summer. She returned with a marked anti-Jewish mindset, and had ascribed to the belief that the problems in Israel were the fault of the Jews. My sister's daughter is at BYU and my sister probably has no idea what her daughter is actually being taught. There is so much unquestioned trust towards the Church when you are on the inside of it, that you never consider questioning what your child may be being taught at BYU or the MTC (Missionary Training Center).

My sons are no longer Mormons. They began declaring to be atheists a couple of years ago. This is very typical of young adult Mormons who leave the Church and realize that they have been used and betrayed by it. They turn against God and anything that looks like Mormonism, including traditional Christianity. Because Mormon churches look like other Christian Churches in many ways, it is normal for former Mormons to reject Christianity. Satan has crafted it this way.

There is a dark occult history of Mormonism that the Mormon Church organization has tried desperately to cover up. Because of the valiant work of Sandra and Gerald Tanner though, they have not been able to completely destroy the true contemptible history of Mormonism. While at the Compassionate Boldness Conference in Utah in 2009, I met Sandra Tanner. I bought her ministry's large book called Mormonism – Shadow or Reality. I spent hours and hours reading this book, as well as other books that contained the truth about the history of Mormonism.

Joseph Smith and his family were into various occult practices[1]. Joseph Smith actually wore a magic talisman around his neck all of his life, including the day he was killed.[2] He was a money digger who was always looking for hidden treasure.[3] There are many affidavits recorded that tell the truth about him and his family. They were considered lazy, indolent, and superstitious people. They had a terrible reputation among the people they lived around.[4] He was not a man anyone could trust. He was practicing adultery before he claimed to get a revelation from God about polygamy.[5] This supposed revelation was "received" in order for him to be able to convince his wife his evil practices were of God.[6] He claimed to have a vision where he saw God and Jesus appear to him as "separate personages".[7] In all reality there are several conflicting accounts of what he supposedly saw, and all are very different.[8] He supposedly used some peep-stone to interpret the Book of Mormon.[9] The Mormon Church still has this stone in their possession.[10] His father was involved with other people who claimed to bear some priesthood that was not of God, but was occult.[11] He was an

40

extremely arrogant man, and claimed that he had been able to keep a church together better than anyone including Jesus Christ.[12] He demanded to be given the wives of all his twelve apostles in solidifying their devotion to him.[13] He was imprisoned for treason charges before he was shot and killed in a gunfight while in Carthage jail.[14] He died at the age of 38 after having been chased from state to state because he would not obey the law of the United States.

My journey into Mormonism seems to have been easy and natural. Nothing about our neighbors gave me any indication of danger. That is actually what makes this organization so dangerous. It has used so much that is beautiful and lovely to lure millions into its silk chains. If one stays in these chains, the end of this path is only eternal damnation. Mormon doctrine carefully leads one away from salvation. It subtly blinds people into a delusion of believing they have been found, when they are so very lost. They enter a world that may hold them and their family members for generations, causing them to not ever realize the eternal consequences of what is taking place.

One of the most difficult parts of my emerging from this darkness has been the memories. I have years of memories of family holidays, vacations, birthdays and other occasions that were ones filled with laughter, love, and life. These have now come to an end. I am no longer welcome at their table. Those memories were undergirded by the fact that all of us were part of a false organization. It provided a lot of emotional "candy," almost like a drug. We were all part of the "Kingdom of God". We had all been "found". We thought that we were all at the Lords' table together. This was all an illusion. What we thought was the Lords' table, was actually a table of demons. We were slowly and carefully and blindly being led to hell, and none of us realized it. Now the only way they can

41

continue in this illusion is to shut me out, and this is what most of them have done.

My daughter, however, has been quite brave. She has, against the counsel and advice of her bishop and my sister, continued to have intermittent contact with me. She has finished her third semester at BYU, and almost two years ago met a young man from Australia who is of Chinese descent. He joined the Mormon Church in Australia over five years ago and is now working on his Master's degree at BYU. One very sad reality is that his parents were both raised in Communist China before immigrating to Australia about thirty years ago. They have sacrificed a lot for their two sons, for them to have better lives than they had in China. What his parents do not realize is that both of their sons have now become a part of an organization that takes away as much freedom as the Communists took from the Chinese people, but they do so headquartered in these United States of America, where freedom reigns more than in any other country on earth. Their sons (the youngest a student at BYU but not yet a member), if they go through the Mormon temple as they are pressured to do, will commit and covenant everything they have, including their lives, to this organization. It will come before everything else in their lives. It will demand a mandatory ten percent tithe, and through the "law of consecration" they will be put under in the temple, they will also promise to give all their money to this organization if they are ever asked to do so. They will be expected to follow the prophet unquestioningly. Any new revelation that the prophet receives they will need to obey. No doubt his parents in Australia are enjoying much more freedom than he is in Utah today.

God has opened doors for us to talk to them, and to share with them some of the truth about the Mormon Church, but those chains are strong. It is our hope that they will not go to the temple to be married this summer like they are now planning to do. I am afraid that if they do, they may be facing years of blindness in this velvet prison. At least they are communicating with us at this time, which has given us the opportunity to reach out to them. When my daughter stayed overnight with me and my husband this summer (she calls our house the "compound" because she is afraid to be there), I was able to show her a DVD about people who were involved with fundamental Mormonism and polygamy and had become Christians. It is called "Lifting the Veil of Polygamy". It was a powerful DVD in relating the heartbreaking stories of these people. It contained their testimonies of God's salvation through grace alone. My daughter had to ask her boyfriend's permission over the phone (her respecting his priesthood) to be able to watch it. He told her to take her Book of Mormon with her into the room, and hold onto it tight so she would not be so afraid. About forty minutes after I started the DVD, the main electrical line outside of our house exploded and made a very loud noise. My husband contacted the power company and they came to fix the line. Each time they tried to fix it though, it would break again in another place, in the end requiring six splices. Eventually, a couple of hours later, we were able to finish watching the DVD. My daughter spent the entire night with the lights on in her room, because she was so terrified about being at our house (so far away from safety in her mind). The next day, however, I could see a small victory had been won. She told her boyfriend over the phone that "her God" (the one I have been trying to teach her about) would not have her practice polygamy. He disagreed of course, as he would follow the prophet and do so out of obedience. Since then we have continued to engage in apologetics with them through letters and emails. He is holding on tightly to the church. We saw them at Christmas for several hours, but it was obvious he felt very uncomfortable around us.

Although I was un-blinded in one day, it has taken over two years now for parts and pieces of the chains of Mormon darkness to fall off or be removed. We live out in the country and have often taken walks in the morning down the country road in front of our house. I remember after my eyes were opened it seemed like day after day I could literally see a little clearer. It was like there had been layers of fog all around me, and slowly they went away. I remember the day when I realized that I did not have to "act" nice all the time. This is when my personality began to emerge. Go to a Mormon Church on any Sunday morning anywhere and you will see a lot of smiles and friendly faces. It is not more than skin deep, however. Through mind control these people's true personalities have been suppressed.

I have seen God work among my family in some amazing ways. At first, my husband and I suffered tremendously as Satan used every opportunity for all of them to come together and lie about us. We have been treated with unkindness, disrespect, disregard and hostility. We have seen how God has turned these things back on Satan's own head, and caused these things to stop. For the past two years now, each time I have spoken with my mother, my daughter, or my two sons, I have prayed intently each time to allow God to direct my thoughts and my words. I was aware that if I was not "wise as a serpent" that lies and slander could begin that might end with both verbal and emotional abuse and even physical abuse. I have learned that I must never respond in kind, but take my pain directly to God and allow Him to transform me, and continue to give me that perfect love for them that I need to have. I would never have believed that the people that I loved the most could be capable of doing

44

and saying the things that they have done and said to me over the past several years. I know how Satan can bring people together against us. But I also know now through experience how God can work in their lives and separate them physically if necessary to keep them from coming together against us.

I attribute all of my survival throughout the experiences of the last few years, and the many years in Mormonism to God alone. I became His child in 1983. My mind had already been heavily influenced by Mormonism since 1972. In my ignorance as a new Christian I did the unthinkable, and with my heart and mind wide open as a born-again believer I became a partaker at the table of demons. God let me know though that someday I would be delivered. He never left me, though I was so far astray. I was His.

My story is one of redemption. God continued to be an unbreakable thread to me from 1983 on throughout my many years as a Mormon. I remember now that when I was in desperate and frightening circumstances, I would repeat words of the hymn "Abide with Me" in my mind. In that hymn the reality that God did not change was spoken of, and I clinged to that truth. As a family we sang the hymn "How Firm a Foundation" probably hundreds of times, including all of the verses. It brought me hope. I was not on a firm foundation at all, but I knew in some way that there was a foundation out there somewhere. I often prayed throughout the years, and was given a quiet assurance that someday everything would make sense. Now it does. God keeps His promises. He said He would never leave us or forsake us. He said that if He started a good work in us that He would complete it until the end. I know these things are true because this has happened to me.

I wrote a poem that describes what I believe God has done for me:

HE CAME FOR ME

I've been redeemed

I've been set free

From the darkest night

God thought of me

The prison walls were high and firm

From chains of steel my soul did yearn

And through the blackest lies of hell

God called to me and the chains they fell

As floods of despair filled my days

And deepest sorrows became my way

God heard my cry and answered me

He let me know I would be free

The maze of demons held me tight

Death had replaced the promised light

Still in the glimmer as my hope did fade

God let me know His plans were laid

Although the master schemer hateful one

Had me bound up tight, in shackles firm

God had another way for me

God had raised that key to set me free

There is no desert God can't see

There is no darkness where He can't be

There is no night He can't make day

There is no demon that can stay

There is no sorrow He can't find

There is no hurting you can hide

There is no gift that you can bring

There is no payment for this King

There is no chain that He can't break

There is no child He can forsake

There is no heart He can't set free

There is no evil that won't flee

There was no other good enough

There is no greater love for us

I've been redeemed

I've been set free

To the deepest hell

God came for me...

I have wasted so many years as a Christian. I can never get back those wasted years. So many dreams that I had have been shattered. They have all fallen to the ground in a desperate pile of ashes. However, as I read certain passages of Isaiah that mention ashes, my heart takes courage. Isaiah 61: 1-3 reads *"The Spirit of the Lord God is upon Me, because the Lord has anointed Me to preach good tidings to the poor; he has sent me to heal the brokenhearted, to proclaim liberty to the captives, and the opening of the prison to those who are bound; to proclaim the acceptable year of the Lord, and the day of vengeance of our God; to comfort all who mourn, to console those who mourn in Zion, to give them beauty for ashes, the oil of joy for mourning, the garment of praise for the spirit of heaviness; that they might be called trees of righteousness, the planting of the Lord, that He may be glorified."*

I am now seeing beauty instead of ashes. I am seeing the light of liberty shine forth; as the true Word of God is spoken to those I love. I am seeing the prison doors being opened and chains of darkness being loosened. This is not done though by me or my husband, but only by God through His Spirit and His Word. We are nothing. He is everything. I have learned that when I am the weakest, the Lord is the strongest, and when my strength falters, His remains. I hope for the rest of my life that He will use me in some small way to bring freedom to so many that are bound by Mormonism and other false religions. There are so many in our world today who, although they live under some amount of freedom granted by a government, they live in chains of Satan because of the lies that they believe about God. True freedom only comes from Jesus Christ. It says in *2 Corinthians 3: 17 Now the Lord is the Spirit; and where the Spirit of the Lord is, there is liberty.*

If we look only to the freedom that our government can give us, we will end up disappointed before much longer. After the rapture of the true church – the born again, blood-bought body of believers, this entire world will come under the government of the Antichrist. He may claim to grant some form of freedom of worship before he requires everyone to worship him. I can see the progressing brainwashing of our culture around us. Many people are beginning now to be prepared for the strong delusion spoken of in Thessalonians. I can see it happening, because it has happened to me. I have worshipped a man - Joseph Smith. This is similar to how those deceived by the Antichrist will worship him.

The only hope that I see for true freedom is in Jesus Christ alone, and nowhere else. It would be wise for us to learn some valuable lessons from the Chinese Christians who have been pressed down for many years under atheistic Communism. They have found their freedom only in Christ. They rely only on Him and little else for everything. They have had no choice. Their freedom comes only from Him. The day may be fast approaching that we have no choice. We can however turn to the one true God in complete submission and dependence upon Him in how we live our lives. I have learned He is mighty to save.

CHAPTER 5

MY RECORD OF LIBERATION

The following journal entries were ones I wrote after emerging from my blindness. These record the daily experiences that I had in coming out from under the powers of darkness into the amazing light of the true God of the Bible.

April 20, 2009

Psalm 6: 2 Have mercy upon me, O Lord; for I am weak: O Lord, heal me; for my bones are troubled.

How do the right roads become the wrong roads so quickly? In one day I saw the error of my ways and how I had allowed myself to be deceived. I had not only allowed myself to be deceived, but all three of my children also. Now, they are suffering for my mistakes.

April 25, 2009

Psalm 30: 2   O Lord my God, I cried out to You, and You healed me.

The Lord has seen that I have made it safely through my journey. So few things have turned out how I would have wanted them to. I know God is in control and I am not. I am learning to trust Him more and more as I accept that I believed many lies for many years. I once believed the Mormon church was the kingdom of God re-established on the earth. I now know that this is a lie. The church is a lie and its leaders are deceiving millions of people.

April 27, 2009

Job 13: 4-5   But you forgers of lies, you are all worthless physicians. Oh, that you would be silent, and it would be your wisdom!

The many times I sought counsel and advice from Mormon Bishops or Stake Presidents! Each time they threw me hurting and bleeding back into the fire. Truly, in the false organization of the Mormon Church, they counsel as foolishly as did Job's friends. They have set themselves up as God's representatives on earth. They are not. They cannot be while they act in accordance with the "kingdom of man," which Joseph Smith established on earth while claiming it to be the "kingdom of God". Christ is no part of the LDS Church, except that He loves the people within it that Satan is so slyly and craftily leading astray.

April 29, 2009

Psalm 82: 5   They do not know, nor do they understand; they walk about in darkness; all the foundations of the earth are unstable.

Now that I see the great deception of the Mormon church, it is all I can do not to want to cry out to so many I know and love that they are being used and deceived by a godless organization governed by men. It robs people of their freedom in Christ, while at the same time claiming to be a church called by the name of Jesus Christ.

April 30, 2009

Psalm 45: 6   Your throne, O God, is forever and ever;   a scepter of righteousness is the scepter of Your kingdom.

How righteous and great is our God! How majestic and wondrous are His works! How beautiful are His creations! In this time when man's creations are all around us, and man's organizations deceive and fail us, how wonderful it is to acknowledge and realize God's greatness! He is never failing and is everlasting! He is our sure hope and foundation! He is our comfort and our eternal Redeemer and Deliverer! Only He knows men's hearts, and the extent of their wickedness. His light can penetrate the deepest, darkest corners and expose Satan's most intricate deceits. God will stand. Satan has been defeated by the atoning sacrifice of Jesus Christ and Satan's works will fall and great will be that fall!

As a Mormon, I have been bound. I have been bound by an organization claiming to be divine. In all reality, however, it is demonic. I was slowly led astray, all in our dear Savior's name. I find it a great affront and offense to my belief in Christ that an organization claiming to be of Christ is anything but "of Christ." I feel more like I am emerging from the mob. My mind was blinded and my heart was deceived. I have raised my children in this deception. After making covenants that I believed were with God, I lived in fear and confusion continually. I can see it all now for what it was and for the ways it held me bound. I hope I can help free others from its awful grasp.

May 7, 2009

Psalm 25: 3 Indeed, let no one who waits on You be ashamed; let those be ashamed who deal treacherously without cause.

Sometimes it feels like I am coming out from behind a cloud. I am waking up from a long, bad dream. Coming out of the Mormon church is a strange experience. Everything that I once thought was white has become black. The entire way that I saw the whole world has changed. I had no clue for years that I was involved in an organization (church) that operates as a cult, that idea was the farthest thing from my mind. I can see now so much more clearly that from around age nine, I associated good feelings and memories with the Mormon church. It seemed like a haven from the trouble I felt in my home, and in my heart, too.

May 12, 2009

Psalm 25: 4 Show me Your ways, O Lord; teach me Your paths.

54

I have much to learn. Since I have been awakened from a long night's sleep inside a false religion, not realizing how cut off from the Lord I had become, life feels new again. The Mormon church is a cult. I was in a cult and was a member of it for twenty-nine years. It influenced everything I did. It influenced the way I saw myself, my marriage, my purpose in life, my children, my extended family, my talents, etc. There is no area of my life that it did not touch in some way. It gave me a false idea of who God was, and what he wanted me to do. It kept me always striving, never reaching, and always feeling guilty. It kept me in bonds and shackles that I had no idea I was in. Having made "sacred" covenants in the temple (the House of the Lord), I felt more than obligated to live up to those covenants, or I would be failing God. When I went through the temple at age 20 in 1984, I vowed to give up my life or "allow" it to be taken if I broke my covenants. One of those covenants was to consecrate everything to the building up of the Church of Jesus Christ of Latter-day Saints on the earth today, or the establishment of the kingdom of God. I was to give everything: time, talent, money – everything which the Lord had blessed me with, and everything which the Lord would bless me with to the church organization – or suffer my life to be taken. Of course all of these covenants were made on my wedding day in the Salt Lake City Temple. I had no idea what I was getting myself into, before I was all the way into it.

May 14, 2009

Psalm 54: 6 I will freely sacrifice to You; I will praise Your name, O Lord, for it is good.

I feel that I have been set free from shackles that have been put around my soul and heart by Mormon doctrine. The more I understand about it in contrast to true

Christianity, the more I realize how pagan and controlling it is. After making blood oaths and covenants in the temple, something occurs. I believe a person's spirit, mind, and heart are all held captive to powerful false beliefs, even without them being consciously aware of it. In a very short time inside the temple, surrounded by other temple patrons, one makes oaths and covenants, the nature of which you are totally unaware of before you go inside. There is brainwashing that goes on in a Mormon church on Sunday, but the brainwashing that goes on inside the temples are on a whole different level. There was a part of the endowment session in the temple where a man representing Satan at the same time represented himself as a preacher. We were consistently led to associate preachers and pastors with Satan, and were taught to be afraid of them. Outside of the temple, in real life, before signing any legal document, one is given the opportunity to know what you are signing and the ramifications of breaking the agreement. In the temple, those receiving their endowments are usually young men or women (such as nineteen year old boys do before leaving home on their two-year missions or twenty-one year old young women if they go on a mission). In the case of a couple being married or "sealed for eternity," they are often young. Fear and control are at the heart of why the Mormon organization has people make covenants in their temples. After making these covenants, they keep you under constant pressure to live up to them, even in order to be able to continue and go and serve in the temples.

May 22, 2009

Psalm 9: 9 The Lord also will be a refuge for the oppressed, a refuge in times of trouble.

How saddened I am by what I am seeing as the blinding shackles of the false religion of Mormonism are falling off. All our emotional and spiritual wounds were covered over and hid so they could not heal. We added wounds to more wounds. How much I wanted to heal and live close to Christ when I came to know Him twenty-six years ago. Unfortunately I had been "bewitched" by false teachers as the Galatians in Paul's day had been. They were also Christians who Paul was trying to protect from false prophets and teachers. Sadly, though, I had no Paul in my life. My Paul (my husband sent into my life by God) did not come along until 2008. He was used by God to bring me out of the darkness and into the light. How hard it was to try and follow Christ and function as a Mormon at the same time. I thought the Mormon church was a place of safety and refuge, but it was instead an unending tunnel of darkness and deception, and I could not see this. Eventually, all I knew was that I was a failure – a failure as a Mormon woman, wife and mother. I could never get it right or right enough at least. When I went to Mormon Priesthood leaders (Bishops or Stake Presidents) seeking counsel and help, I was thrown back into a maze of "I'm just not doing enough" time after time. It was always my fault somehow. I was never being a good enough Mormon.

June 5, 2009

Psalm 29: 11   The Lord will give strength to His people; the Lord will bless His people with peace.

As the Mormon church does not use the cross as a symbol of their Jesus Christ, they teach a false Jesus Christ. The Jesus of Mormonism expects his followers to do ALL he or she can do to be righteous, BEFORE any of his "mercy" will apply in their lives. Instead of the LDS church bringing freedom to people by leading them to the Jesus Christ of the Bible, to His great and bountiful mercy and grace, they place tremendous loads and burdens on people that they cannot bear. The rate of depression in Utah is much higher than in other states. Suicide rates among young men are also much higher in Utah than in other states. Following the Mormon Jesus often leads to depression and despair.

Mormons would say they are persecuted because the true Church of Christ is always persecuted. No, true Christians in many parts of the world are the ones that have been, and are being persecuted and killed for their faith. God gives these Christians the grace that they need to go through such things. Church organizations, such as the Catholic Church have persecuted and killed people they see as being heretics to their organizations. This Mormon persecution complex only serves to further bind and blind people into believing that they are suffering for Christ's sake – No, they are suffering for Satan's sake. Jesus Christ came to set us free through His love and mercy. He would not put such heavy loads on His followers that they would break down in despair. He is a loving and a good God. He said "My yoke is easy and My burden is light". Only Satan's burden is not easy, and an organization attempting to hold itself up as a "Church of Jesus Christ" that would bind people and lay burdens on them that they cannot bear, cannot be of God, but only of Satan.

June 8, 2009

Psalm 66: 12 You have caused men to ride over our heads; we went through fire and through water; but You brought us out to rich fulfillment.

As my eyes have been opened to the truth about the Mormon Church, in my frustration I wrote a formal indictment against them as I consider the great price of my association with the church over many years. I know they will never be held accountable in men's courts, but all judgments are in God's hands.

I, Shawna Kay Lindsey, do hereby formally accuse the above mentioned organization of deception of the highest order. This organization along with its leaders both dead and living have violated the sacred laws of God in that they have set themselves up to be a light unto men while in all reality being full of darkness. Their founders are falsely revered because truth has been carefully and intentionally hidden from those caught in the trap of this satanic organization. For almost two hundred years this organization has placed unsuspecting and innocent souls under chains and bonds through false oaths and covenants. This organization has blasphemed the sacred name of Jesus Christ by teaching and preaching another gospel, one satanically crafted to bind and snare people with false scripture inspired by none other than Satan himself. This organization is responsible for the murder of innocent men, women and children. It is responsible for raising fornication and adultery in the form of polygamy, to an act falsely claimed to be sanctioned of God. It has caused the lives of countless people to be slowly used up in supposed service to God, while in all actuality they have been in service to the father of lies and the prince of this world. This organization and its false priesthood bearing leaders have taken unrighteous dominion over the lives of thousands of missionaries deluded into believing they are engaged in the Lord's work ,while they have become bearers of lies and falsehoods. Thousands of women and children have become victims of verbal, physical, and sexual abuse because of the polygamous lifestyles which many people entered into following the perverted example and direction of Joseph Smith and Brigham Young.

Personally this organization has led me and my children away from Jesus Christ. Through blood oaths and covenants that I was deceived into believing were sacred covenants; I was entangled in demonic chains which tightly bound my heart and mind for over twenty-five years. I lived in tremendous fear of breaking those covenants because I foolishly believed they were of God.

June 9, 2009

Psalm 92: 13   Those who are planted in the house of the Lord shall flourish in the courts of our God.

Sometimes the sorrow over so many years of being deceived almost completely overwhelms me. All I wanted to do was raise my children to know and follow Jesus. This did not happen, and as they are now young adults, it is more evident than ever. Being in the Mormon church gave us a false idea of who we were supposed to be as individuals and as a family, as well as what we were supposed to do. There is very little room within the "kingdom of God" to fail. There is no salvation for those who leave the church. The church falsely claims the ability to grant people eternal life, and to send them to outer darkness or eternal damnation. Since I was once an "endowed" member of the church with a full knowledge of the "restored" gospel, and have now turned away, I am the worst of the worst – a daughter of perdition. I am so grateful though that the Lord Jesus Christ is my judge, and not a false organization crafted by wicked and deceiving men. Jesus will judge me, and He is the perfect omnipotent one and only loving God of all creation.

Slowly the false ideas and doctrines that I believed are being replaced by the pure doctrines of the living Word of God – the Bible. These doctrines come to me now like cool clean water to one who has wandered in the desert of false belief for over half a life. My spiritual bones are weak and brittle, and I find truth nourishing me like new bone marrow strengthens someone with a weak frame. Over the years in the Mormon church, I met many women who were suffering from depression, loneliness, various types of abuse, as well as the constant reality that they could never measure up to the standards set by the church. There was the double bind: fail the church – fail God – then where can you turn? Satan often had them in a vice grip of despair. Until they looked outside the box – outside of the "Lord's church", where the church forbad them to go, they were bound and trapped. There is no teaching or understanding of grace in Mormonism. If grace is spoken about, it is not biblical grace. There are teachings against anyone being in paid ministry which is considered "priestcraft" in the Book of Mormon and is seen to be of Satan. Mormons are subtly taught to be afraid to listen to preachers, for fear of being led astray by them. Sadly they are not aware that they have already been led astray by false teachers.

About ten years after becoming active in the Mormon Church and being married in the temple, I began seeing myself and my family as the "walking wounded". We were doing all the Church was telling us to do to please God, but we were becoming more and more depleted and exhausted emotionally and spiritually. We found it harder and harder to be able to present ourselves as a "faithful Mormon family," who were being so "blessed" by the restored gospel. Though believing Mormons would disagree, the Mormon church leaders are always pressuring church members to have a "form" of godliness, while in all reality denying the power thereof. They pervert who Jesus Christ truly is and load burdens upon church members' backs regarding what God would have them do.

June 12, 2009

Psalm 54: 2 Hear my prayer, O God; give ear to the words of my mouth.

Tremendous false burdens are placed upon the backs and minds of the Latter-Day-Saints. Their Jesus Christ is a god that will grant them mercy only after all they can do themselves for their own salvation. You are continually striving to be good enough, perfect enough, pure enough, and righteous enough...so that you may rest. But there is never really any rest; you must "endure to the end".

I woke up this morning praying that I may "serve" God. Then I began thinking that I have not heard much about this in the past year while learning more about true Christianity. As a Mormon, you are always encouraged to "serve" God. As if he will never be satisfied. You are led to believe that you must continually be sacrificing yourself for him. He then becomes a god that in some way is always lacking. We were expected continually by him to give him everything we have. This concept opposes who Jesus Christ really is. Jesus – God Himself – is complete in who He is. He is the all-powerful, all-knowing, all-loving Creator of the universe who is Sovereign in Himself. He is not looking for sacrifices from us for Him to be appeased, like a pagan god always requiring greater and greater sacrifices from his followers. Satan, the father of lies is the one actually receiving worship when one serves a pagan god. Satan is never satisfied, and always wants to take away as much as he can from his followers. Throughout the ages people have offered even human sacrifices to pagan gods. Satan is behind such practices, and is delighted at the perversion and misery he is causing.

I had no idea that the pagan god of Mormonism that I was serving was none other than Satan himself. The true and living God would never have had me enter into an oath and covenant at twenty years old where I am required "in front of God, angels, and these witnesses" to draw my hand quickly under my throat displaying the manner that my life would be taken if I revealed or broke these "sacred" covenants. That god is none other than Satan himself. The Creator of the universe and Creator of our souls and Him Who gave Himself as the perfect sacrifice for the sins of all mankind would never expect His children to enter into such covenants, only Satan would. The perfect atoning sacrifice of Jesus Christ is dismissed in Mormonism and replaced by a teaching that requires one to atone for their own sins if need be. Where is the mercy and grace of the Mormon Jesus? The mercy and grace of the Mormon Jesus requires everything, maybe even one's own life, before any mercy is shown. The simple gospel message that God reached down to us in the form of His Son, and was born into this world of a virgin mother into humble circumstances, lived a perfect sinless life and became our Savior is twisted and changed by the Mormon church into a false gospel that is actually one that craftily leads its members into bondage to Satan, while at the same time they believe they are serving God.

Recently, I asked my sons' forgiveness for raising them in a cult. My heart's intentions were opposite to what actually took place. I had wanted them to come to know the Jesus Christ I had accepted as my personal Savior in 1983. How great the price that must be paid for following Satan and not God. It is a miracle that we all made it through these experiences, at least still physically alive.

June 16, 2009

Psalm 53: 6   Oh, that the salvation of Israel would come out of Zion! When God brings back the captivity of His people, let Jacob rejoice and Israel be glad.

Two mornings ago I fell apart after praying out loud with my husband. I am aware so much now how I am trying to understand the true nature of God, not the god of Mormonism. The god of Mormonism prefers to be addressed with the words "thee", "thou", and "thy". The god of Mormonism was once a man, and is now exalted. The true God is so much bigger and comprehensive. Mormon doctrine teaches of a god who requires so much before showing any mercy. He is a god who enslaves and demands perfection. There is no room for error.

Throughout my twenty-nine years in the Mormon Church, I came to know many women that were worn out and depressed. There was no way that they could do all the church was requiring them to do. One woman had eleven children. She was the Relief Society President for our ward, and she was also the PTA president at her children's elementary school, and was teaching part-time at the university (she had a master's degree). The Mormon women I met who were not able to have children suffered tremendously in the Mormon Church. So much of a Mormon woman's identity is related to being a mother. Those women who could not have children really struggled to feel that God loved them as much as He did others who were having many children. I met many women who were on anti-depressants. They could hardly take care of themselves, and were literally "sacrificing" their emotional and mental health for their families, and for the building up of the "Kingdom of God" on the earth.

At least four or five women I knew in the Mormon Church were diagnosed as manic-depressive and put on medication. I also knew many women who would go to their Bishops or Stake President Leaders for help, only to be told to just pray and read their scriptures more, and exercise more faith.

June 17, 2009

Psalm 100: 3 Know that the Lord, He is God; it is He who has made us, and not we ourselves; we are His people and the sheep of His pasture.

There are many well-educated and talented people who are Mormons. Over the years as a Mormon, we met doctors, dentists, professors, engineers, teachers, and musicians, professional athletes, etc. If they went to the temple, they all covenanted to give everything for the building up of the Lord's Kingdom, even their lives if required. Why would the god of Mormonism require so much? The true God sacrificed Himself for us to offer us eternal life. As a Mormon, one's focus becomes completely what God requires us to do, not what he has done for us. If one becomes a Mormon and follows all the precepts of the church, this automatically creates a "form of godliness". However, without a true conversion or born again experience, where one accepts that he is a sinner and gives his heart to Jesus Christ as his personal Savior, there is only an outward change in behavior, the heart remains the same. Truly no saving grace comes into effect without trusting in one's heart what Jesus has done for us. The longer I was in the church, the more it was about being a good Mormon. The more it was about being a good Mormon, the less I felt connected to the church.

As a Mormon, one is led to believe that all good things come from the church or the "Kingdom of God" – and if you leave this organization, that you will lose ALL your blessings – because it would be turning against God Himself. This is nothing but despicable fear tactics used to keep people under the control of this organization.

Mental and emotional problems often become covered up and buried when you are a committed Mormon. To satisfy the requirements of the organization becomes the top priority in one's life. It is the gift that keeps on taking. Suffering may become a way of life. Sacrifice and pain seem commonplace. Some of the most troubled and confused people who have come out of broken families end up in cults. Often they are people who are seeking love and acceptance. They are generally insecure and in denial of their real emotions before they go into the cult. The cult comes along offering them a new version of reality that may appear to make sense somehow. Within the cult you are given a warped sense of who you are, and an even more warped sense of who God is. Many people are often "love-bombed" into a cult and shown an inordinate amount of attention by other cult members, so that that person will begin to feel he or she is a part of another family (the church family).

When I look back over the years I spent in the church I wonder how I could have been blinded for so long. I wonder why I suffered so much and did so much, both inside and outside the church. I was not living the life God had created me to live. The last ten years I was in the church, I could no longer sing in the choir, even though I loved to sing. My heart had been put in chains. I could not remember people's names in our ward. I could not feel comfortable at church, or being involved in the Young Women's organization. I felt guarded around fellow Mormons all the time. I never felt like I could be myself. I know now that my heart was trying hard to break free of the lies of Mormonism. My mind was still indoctrinated, but slowly Mormonism was losing its' grip on my heart. My heart was hurting terribly and was filled with disappointment and confusion. Over these years my marriage unraveled. My heart continued to break over the discrepancy I felt in what I wanted my life to be, and actually what it was. I wanted to feel the peace that I had felt when I first accepted Jesus as my Savior years before.

June 19, 2009

Psalm 85: 7 Show us Your mercy, Lord, and grant us Your salvation.

It is said that churches that abuse are institutions of denial. I also became an institution of denial in my own way while in the Mormon church. More than ever, I realize now how little I dealt with the traumas and challenges that occurred while I was inside the church. I have cried about the car accident we had in 1995 one time in fourteen years. We had a serious head-on collision leaving our seven year-old son with a brain injury. Now, years later, I am slowly opening up and allowing emotions to emerge on their own.

Mostly, things after the car accident seemed okay. We barely missed a beat (a sign that something was definitely wrong – we did no grieving). I remember feeling confused about why things appeared to be falling apart (various challenges coming into our lives). Weren't we doing what the Lord wanted us to be doing is what I thought. Weren't we keeping our covenants and attending the temple regularly? Weren't we striving to do all we could do for the building up of the "Kingdom of God"? We were, and it was killing us. There was not any time for recovery or rest. No time for tears or grief. Wasn't suffering just part of the plan? Weren't these things just making better "latter-day saints" of us? The happy family veneer that the church "encourages" you to always portray was being sheared off of us through the challenges that came into our lives. Underneath that veneer lie two very damaged and hurting adults, and three confused children who fortunately had survived a horrible car accident.

July 1, 2009

Psalm 71: 3   Be my strong refuge, to which I may resort continually;   You have given the commandment to save me, for You art my rock and my fortress.

I recognize now how Mormonism takes a person's personality and a person's identity away. You become a self-sacrifice for a false god. Your life becomes only a reflection of your commitment to be controlled by the church, and its teachings. Everything else becomes secondary. Your identity as a Mormon, overrides your identity as a person. YOU serve the image. It does not serve you. YOU and YOUR dreams are sacrificed for "higher" causes, the preeminent cause being the organization of the church.

Many early Mormon pioneers gave up their lives while crossing the western plains in the dead of winter on their way to Utah. Most felt they were doing this for God. Why else would they have put themselves and their children through such horrendous situations and conditions? The true God of the Bible was not guiding them to Utah, as many of them were deluded into thinking. In reality, they were being run out of the boundaries of America because of their not obeying the laws of the land, especially regarding the practice of polygamy.

As I look back over my years in the church, I now realize that the way I saw myself, my marriage and my children was completely distorted. The way I saw God was distorted. My judgment was impaired. My value system was altered. The way I saw everyone was warped. My understanding of myself was completely unrealistic. My life was not my own.

So many concepts I am learning about today are new concepts for me. Trust is probably the greatest one. Trusting God and trusting others is vital, but it is still difficult. I wish I could just snap my fingers and the fog and remnants of my chains would disappear, but this is not the case. Slowly, day by day things are getting better. My heart, mind and spirit are healing. I am becoming whole. There are moments, however, when I am overcome with despair. Thoughts of the years that I seem to have wasted, nearly completely engulf me with sadness. I pray often and ask God to carry these things when they overwhelm me. Looking back and clearly seeing, out from under the blindness I was under for so long, hurts. There is no way around it though. I cannot run away from it, and I cannot pretend it all did not happen. I must look at the mirror of the Word of God, and see where all the cracks and broken pieces of me and my life are. I can no longer ignore the truth.

July 4, 2009

Psalm 79: 9   Help us, O God of our salvation, for the glory of Your name: and deliver us, and provide atonement for our sins, for Your name's sake!

I feel sweet freedom in so many ways. This is the first Fourth of July I have spent in twenty-nine years not being a Mormon. "My chains are gone, I've been set free". My heart is emerging from its long night of darkness. My soul is slowly arising to a true and lasting understanding of who God is, and how great He is. I have been a prisoner of a false god, who is none other than Satan himself. It has nearly destroyed me and those I love. The end goal of Satan, or any false god that he deceives us to follow, is only death and destruction. There is only one way to salvation, and that is through Jesus Christ and His saving blood. As culturally and politically incorrect as this may be today, it is true. If one believes in a god that is false, then one will live a life that is false. Following a false god will only bring blindness. Jesus Christ brought living water and gave Himself for us so we would not be eternally separated from Him (not asking for us to sacrifice ourselves for our own salvation). False gods ask for sacrifices that only torture, bind, and blind. The only true and living God has given His life for us, so we can come to Him broken and bruised, and be healed.

July 6, 2009

Psalm 83: 18   That they may know that You, whose name alone is the Lord, are the Most High over all the earth.

I want more than anything else to know God and understand His ways. My desire is to come to trust Him with all my heart and follow His Spirit.

There was a false security in living life while believing in a false god. As a Mormon I was told constantly to "follow the Spirit", supposedly God's Spirit. However, this spirit that was spoken of in the church would not allow us to look outside of the box of the church. It was a false and lying spirit or spirits that were binding me to the doctrines of Mormonism. It is not the true Spirit of God that is spoken about in the Mormon church. The Priesthood in the Mormon church claims to have the authority to lay hands on someone's head after baptism and confer the gift of the Holy Ghost. I would venture to say that this is not the gift of the Holy Ghost, but the gift of an unholy spirit that they give. Only God indwells us with His Holy Spirit. This is a work that only God does. Man does not have the authority to control the Spirit of the Almighty God. The true Spirit of God that I had indwelling me had come from my accepting Jesus Christ as my personal Savior in 1983. I had been given the "gift" of another spirit after I was baptized into the Mormon Church in 1979. God had, through His Holy Spirit, placed a down payment on me in 1983. He would not ever leave me or forsake me, because I was His. Although it took years for me to realize the error of my ways, He did not let go of me. I was His. I had been bought and paid for by His blood. I did not understand this over these years, but He did. When anyone accepts Jesus Christ as their Savior and experiences regeneration, they belong to God and nothing can snatch them out of His hands. I know this to be true. What an amazing thing it has been for me to come to the understanding of the permanence of salvation. I was not holding on to Him, He was holding on to me. I did not understand much about who He was. The wolves had entered my life before I was saved, and I allowed them to reenter my life shortly after I was saved by going back to the Mormon church. This is a common occurrence in the New Testament. Satan sends his false teachers after new believers. I needed a "Paul" in my life. Eventually God sent one.

Even though the Mormon church claims that they care so much about families, this is an absolute lie. This is revealed by what happens in the family when one person leaves the church and openly renounces its teachings. Satan may cause an enormous rift in those relationships. He will bring emotional torture to the person leaving the church, through bitterness and lies that may be spread about that person. They will often be shunned and banished from their families and friends. Many Mormons actually know the church is a lie, but they feel trapped because they know that they will suffer divorce and broken relationships if they are honest and leave the church.

With the delusion that Satan gives, along with the false doctrine of Mormonism, families are often unaware of serious problems that may be occurring within their families. If you look just below the surface of what may appear to be healthy Mormon families, you will find instead problems with abuse, pornography, homosexuality, etc. The delusional blindness that operates inside the church keeps a person from clearly seeing what is really going on within a family. I know that over the years in the church, I saw many emotional and psychological problems within Mormon families, as well as in my own family. The worst case of sexual abuse in Northern Georgia that was prosecuted in the district attorney's office that I spent time working in several years ago occurred in a Mormon family in my sister's ward. A counselor in a bishopric confessed to molesting all five of his children. I was told by the prosecutor that in his fifteen years as a prosecutor, this case was the worst case of child molestation that he had ever seen. Those people in the ward, and those in this man's family seemed completely oblivious to this having gone on for many years.

It is my belief when you are being dominated by a lying spirit; you deceive others about who you are, without even realizing you are doing so. I have come to recognize that I often felt compelled outwardly to "act nice" when that was not at all what I was feeling inside. I now can often recognize people who are in cults, Mormon or others, by the way they communicate. They often seem too "nice". It is as if their real feelings have been suppressed, and something else is driving their emotions. I distinctly remember the day when I realized I did not have to "act nice" anymore. I was realizing that I could just be me. It sounds like common sense, but to those who have had their personalities taken away and given over to Satan; it is amazing to come out from under this. Many times I have shared with my husband that it is like coming out of a fog, or having layers of shadows lifted from me. I actually have come to literally see and experience everything differently.

July 13, 2009

Psalm 92: 12   The righteous shall flourish like a palm tree: he shall grow like a cedar in Lebanon.

True and lasting peace and freedom only come from knowing and following the one true living God. There is no other way. The way is narrow, for it is only by Him that we can be saved and NOT of ourselves. I know this is true. I know this, but so many that I love are still walking in darkness, and are blinded by false spirits and believe a false gospel. They cannot hear with their ears and see with their eyes. They have bought a fraud and are captured and enslaved by him who would destroy their souls. He will starve them with a lack of truth, and whisper to them that they are doing the right thing. He will slowly and carefully administer a diet of poison to them without them realizing it. He will grip them with claws of fear that will hold them in place like helpless animals that are caught in a trap. They may suffer for years, and live lives of weary desperation. They may ignore what is in their hearts for the lies that are in their heads. They will feed their children on empty bones and lead them into prison and chains. They may continue to show outwardly a form of godliness, while denying the power thereof. If they awaken one day, and see clearly who they have actually been serving, they will see that they have also become weak, trapped, and helpless. They also will realize their children are starving and dying, and that their false dreams are entwined with Satan's schemes. They will also see that they may have lived a "religious" life, but not a Spirit-filled life. They will also find themselves measured and found wanting. They may also feel as Solomon did, that all is vanity and without meaning. They may also see that their paths have been paths to death and not to life. They will also see that they never could have saved themselves, and that it was a grand waste of time trying. They will also see that he who deceived them, will not save them. They will also be abandoned, alone, and empty. They will also see that promises of the evil one only turn to ashes. The places that they once saw as beautiful will become what they really are, places where demons dwell. They will also find at the end of this road, there is no lasting peace. They will also see that they are filled with wounds that are not healed, and that these wounds have been left unattended and festering for years. They will also see that this false god will only have taken from them, and will throw them away in an instant. How my heart has broken for so many I love and care about who have been ravaged by this false religion. Satan truly is cursed above all other creatures and his destiny is unfathomable darkness.

How grateful I am for light, for the true light of Jesus Christ who gives life and gives it so abundantly. How grateful I am to have His Word to read. I know it is powerful, sharper than a two-edged sword. He is the King of Kings and Lord of Lords. He alone is worthy of all praise, honor, and glory. There is no other above Him. He clears our way and removes the traps and snares of the evil one. He restores us to Himself in all fullness of life. He is our only shield and is the protector of our souls. Only He can guide us in wisdoms' paths. He hears our cries and answers our prayers. He gives us comfort that the world knows not of. He alone can bind up our hearts and give our minds soundness. He alone teaches us all good things. He alone gives us breath and extends our days. He brings us through great floods of darkness, and carries us away from evil. He plants us on a firm foundation, which is none other than Himself in all His majesty and glory. His Spirit alone, through His Word, teaches us all truth, and gives us the discernment we need. He alone carries us through the deepest valleys of sorrow and gives us joy in the morning. He removes fear far from us and causes us to stand.

July 15, 2009

Psalm 106: 12-13 Then they believed His words; they sang His praise. They soon forgot His works; they did not wait for His counsel.

How my cowardly heart wants to flee from this place, this place of truth that brings such painful reality to me. It seems that I would like to run a hundred miles in any direction to not be here. I must be honest, this is how I feel. I cannot run away though. This is where I am supposed to be. I ran for years through the storms, now I feel the storms run through me. Although now I know that God is carrying me, helping me not to be obliterated by them. I wish I was not such a coward. God has been so gracious to me in bringing me to this place. When we see ourselves in complete naked helplessness before God, it is uncomfortable to say the least. It rips us apart down to the very deepest parts of our souls, and exposes how we are nothing before an Almighty God. When we are being shaped by the Father of the universe and the One and only Savior of mankind, it burns as no other fire can burn. It burns us until nothing is left of us, except that which He can use for His purposes. It is only by the grace of God that I am here writing these things today. My strength has fallen to nothing. My foolishness is so obvious to me in so many ways. Too many times I wish I had been able to fall into the arms of Jesus but I did not, now that I understand who He really is I can do this. I have tried to rely on myself so much, and I have failed. God has overcome, I have not.

None of us can or will escape the piercing eyes of Almighty God. He knows all and sees all. There is no other beside Him. Now I find myself growing smaller, and God becoming so much greater. I understand so little, and there is so much I need to learn. Who can run away from God? He will find you.

July 23, 2009

Psalm 107: 9 For He satisfies the longing soul, and fills the hungry soul with goodness.

I feel so blessed to have calm in the storm, which has been my life, or so it seems. As my eyes open, I am so sad to see the effect the Mormon church has had on my children. I so wrongly thought that I was going in a direction that they could follow. Little did I realize that I was on a dead end road, leading to nowhere. It is as if I have been swimming underwater for years, and have finally emerged at the surface of the water, and see that I am no farther than where I began years ago when I became a Mormon at the age of sixteen. At least now, though, I know where I can find air to breathe. God has ultimately brought me to this place in my life. It is my hope and prayer that my experience as a Mormon will somehow help others. I often wonder why I was not brought out of my blindness earlier. I wonder why other Christians that I met through the years did not shake me and wake me. It is all I can do now, seeing what God has brought me out of, to not try to jerk those I love out of the fire. God is telling me, however, that this must be done in His way and His time. It feels to me today that I am on a battlefield, and can see so many I love and care about lying wounded around me, and I cannot reach them and help them. They cannot even see how they are wounded, lost, and deceived.

It seems that we often attempt to stand ourselves up, but inevitably fall down again. We don't ask for help from the only one who really knows where we are, what condition we are in, and what needs to take place for us to be healed. How foolish we often are in being God's creatures, and not seeking help from our Creator. True and lasting healing can only come from God, who knows exactly how to help us. About eleven years ago I gave up trying to turn to others for guidance. I knew my wounds were too deep to be taken care of by someone. I needed help that only God could give. It seemed that most people around me were too lost to help me find my way. That was actually true.

I wasted days, weeks, months, and years lying to myself that I had everything under control. I had nothing under control. I wasted way too much time trying to control others. I tried to be the master of my own life. It is impossible. It does not work. We were created by God, and only He is to be the Master of our lives. Until we come to realize and accept this, we live very small and lie to ourselves. We were created to have a personal relationship with Jesus Christ. This is what He wants for us, and He will take His rightful place as Master of our lives if we allow Him. He is a gentleman, though. He will not force us. Only the truth, His truth, sets us free.

July 24, 2009

Psalm 116: 7   Return to your rest, O my soul; for the Lord has dealt bountifully with you.

Only God has brought me to this place. I know and understand now that He has been there for me, even though I was so lost in false beliefs. He seemed so far away though, not because of Him, but because of my bad choices. He was always there, and I could feel His presence when I drew near to him in my loneliness, confusion, and sorrow. He did give me comfort when no one else could, though I mistakenly continued to follow after the false god of Mormonism and thought I was doing His will.

It is never enough if we are clean on the outside, but inside there is poison and decay. God wants to clean us up from the inside out. It is never enough to only have a "form" or "appearance" of godliness. God looks upon our hearts. We cannot hide our hearts from Him. I can see now, through hindsight, that as a very new Christian I wanted to hold to the false Mormon doctrine that told me I had a father in heaven who loved me. I did have a Heavenly Father who loved me, but I had only become His child after accepting and trusting Jesus Christ as my Savior. I had not become a child of God before I came to earth, as the Mormon Church teaches. They tried to tell me what I needed to do to please my Father in heaven. I think I was especially vulnerable to these lies because of my unhealthy relationship with my father. More than anything I wanted the love of a father. The Mormon "Father in Heaven" became the father I had never known. He became the father that loved me perfectly in a "chaste" way. He became to me that father that would never harm me. I remember being overwhelmed with feelings that I finally had a father that loved me. I only wanted to please him. This false "Father in Heaven" filled that void deep within my heart and mind with lies, that he would give me the love I so desperately wanted, IF I would covenant with him to give everything to him, even my life. I was especially snared because of my lack of a strong relationship with my own father. In my mind and heart, I replaced my father with this new "Father in Heaven" of Mormonism. The main problem with all of this is that the "Father in Heaven" of Mormonism is not the true and living God of the Bible. The Mormon "Father in Heaven" is so much smaller and so needy. My journey out of Mormonism has been one of letting go of this false "Father in Heaven" and coming to know my true Creator and Redeemer, Jesus Christ.

It is like I had settled for such a small god, and did not know it. The Mormon Church offered something like a fancy decorated cake that when you cut into it, only decay and rottenness came out. Satan has crafted within various cults the false idea that one has been "found", when really one is not only lost but also "falsely found". When one is falsely found, you may not realize how lost you really are. We don't seek to be "found" when we don't know we are lost. This is the tragedy of false beliefs; people think that they have been found, and don't have a clue how lost they really are. Satan tries to lull us to sleep in deceiving us to believe that our lives are somehow enough. When we think that we are beautiful enough, successful enough, good enough to merit something ourselves, we are being deceived. There is nothing we can do for our salvation. Jesus did it ALL. Who needs a savior if they are continually thinking that they are enough in themselves? God wants to meet us in our brokenness. It is finally becoming to me okay NOT to be okay. This comes as such a new concept for me. As a Mormon my whole focus was always on what I was doing (with a capital 'I') to please god, and not on what God was doing in my life.

Jesus was sought while on this earth by those people who were hurting, and knew they were hurting. What did the Pharisees or Sadducees need from Him? Their focus was all on what they were doing, not what Jesus could do for them. Only the broken come to know His true power and greatness. Only those that hungered were fed. Only those that thirsted were given that new and living water.

July 27, 2009

Psalm 119: 71 It is good for me that I have been afflicted; that I may learn Your statutes.

Now that I realize how deceived I was for so many years, it is difficult for me to trust at all. I do not trust myself. If I was led astray once, it seems like I could be led astray again. I only want to learn whatever I need to learn from this costly experience. Satan will try and deceive us no matter how good and sincere our desires may be. I wanted with all my heart to know and please God. I wanted to raise my children to know and love Him. I have failed. God has not.

I have learned that the Spirit of God prays for us when we do not know what to pray for, or how to pray. I spent many years, about the past fourteen years praying "Lord, Your will be done, not mine". All I knew at the time was that everything seemed to be coming apart, and I could not understand why. I felt a constant sense of desperation, along with a little hope that someday everything would make more sense to me. Now many things are making sense. God heard and answered my prayers. He truly does not forsake His children.

In the kingdom of this world, in Satan's kingdom, there is no room for brokenness. The more broken we became as a family, the less worthy we felt of God's love. This is not the case with the true God. He welcomes our brokenness, because He can then be our Healer. Satan ultimately destroys his own. When Satan fails someone, he fails them completely.

The story the Church of Jesus Christ of Latter-day Saints sold me, became the fairy tale which now my nightmares are made of. When a person is emerging from a cult, experiencing nightmares is common. I have had many of them. I will admit that I have also been "haunted" continually with a spirit of fear. Several days pass by, and another layer of deception comes off and I realize how I am a little less afraid. I have read that coming out of a cult takes actually about three years. My blindness was lifted in a day, but the residual effects of the brainwashing and indoctrination have continued to trouble me. Each day it becomes a little easier. I have been troubled at times though with extreme sadness, and at times even thoughts of suicide.

The last six or seven years as a family while still going to church, it seems we fed off each other. We had no peace whatsoever. We felt worthless. In the end it is like Satan chewed us up and spit us out like garbage not fit to be burned. We felt like we had failed the "Lord's church," and what do you do if you fail God. So many people who have realized the Mormon church is a sham, unless they come to know the true God and receive His grace, they become very bitter atheists. This is common. Both of my sons became professing atheists several years after leaving the church. It looks so much on the outside like true Christianity that many ex-Mormons often reject Christianity because it reminds them of Mormonism. Much of the language used in Mormonism is the same used in Christianity; but the meaning of the words is changed.

I find that certain words like "covenant", "temple", and "sacrament" cause me to have negative physical reactions when I hear them. Words like these, which remind me of Mormonism, now carry such a negative connotation, that I repel when I hear them. This is getting better over time though. The last thing I wanted to do when I realized the Mormon church was a huge lie, was to go back into a church. It was like I wanted to run away from anything and everything that reminded me of Mormonism. Fortunately the music that is sung in the church I go to now is not the same music I sang in the Mormon Church. This has been very refreshing and healing. I also felt very lost when I first started to go to the large Baptist church we go to now, because it seemed so free. I was subconsciously looking for walls, and was finding none. I was also looking for roles to play, but there were none. People were just who they were. This was refreshing, but confusing too. It felt sort of like I had transitioned from a communist system to democracy. Freedom was refreshing, but a little frightening too.

Needless to say, I was lost for quite some time. I spent a lot of time just observing, and not really participating much.

July 28, 2009

Psalm 119: 34 Give me understanding, and I shall keep Your law; Indeed, I shall observe it with my whole heart.

Meeting my husband in April of 2008 started the process of my emerging from the darkness. He was not satisfied with me believing the Mormon Church was true.

He challenged me to put the Book of Mormon down, and just read the New Testament. I did this for a year before the blindness of false doctrine fell from my eyes. We had many discussions, and at times hours of arguments over doctrine. All this time, though, I was beginning to see by the power of God through His Word, how wrong I was. God sent me the right man who was strong enough in his faith not to back down. I am so grateful for his faith and perseverance. It changed my life. Often it takes boldness when dealing with people who believe so much false doctrine. My husband was bold. He needed to be. Ultimately, however, it was the Word of God that cut through the entangled web of lies and deception in my mind and heart. Only God's Word can do this, nothing else can.

July 30, 2009

Jeremiah 3: 25 We lie down in our shame, and our reproach covers us. For we have sinned against the Lord our God, we and our fathers, from our youth even to this day, and have not obeyed the voice of the Lord our God.

As I just read from the book of Jeremiah in the Bible, I read that his broken heart caused him to write a broken book. I believe this is what I am doing. I have been writing straight from a broken heart. It seems that my heart has been releasing emotion in waves. I am healing more and more as I write what I am going through.

I am going to be baptized this coming Sunday. I had been baptized into the Mormon Church in 1979. This, however, was not a believer's baptism. I now understand baptism to be an outward sign of a having given your life to Jesus Christ. It is not just a way to join a church. It is not essential to salvation. I have not been baptized as a believer, and now it is time to be baptized.

I recently started reading a book about a young girl who was a Christian growing up in Nazi Germany. It is called Hansi – The Girl Who Loved the Swastika. She was a young, Christian teenage girl who was selected to attend a Nazi school in Prague. As a Christian, she was brainwashed to follow Hitler and his atheistic beliefs. As I read about her experiences living in Nazi Germany, they are eerily similar to my years in the Mormon Church. She was led to worship Hitler as a god[15]. I believe I was led to worship Joseph Smith. There is no praise music in the Mormon Church. One hymn however is entitled "Praise to the Man". It refers to Joseph Smith, and what he did. He is praised in the church. The current prophet is praised in the church. Ultimately, as a Mormon, everyone is becoming a "god," so they really end up worshipping themselves. The idea of exaltation to godhood is taught in Mormonism as something that "our Heavenly Father" would want for his children. How foolish this is. It is Satan that wanted to be like God, and ascend to the throne of God and be worshipped as God.

July 31, 2009

Jeremiah 5: 26   For among my people are found wicked men; they lie in wait as one who sets snares; they set a trap; they catch men.

I was caught in a trap for years that had been set by wicked men. Men in the Mormon church are given the priesthood or the "power to act in the name of God upon the earth." The bare truth is that Jesus Christ is our Great high Priest, He and He alone. He has not left any organized priesthood to act in His name upon the earth. Actually, we all become priests through being indwelt by His Holy Spirit. Man does not act in God's name upon this earth, but God acts by drawing people to Himself and indwelling them through His Holy Spirit. To claim to have priesthood authority that has not been given by God, means that man is only acting in his own authority, not through any authority from God.

How much more I know about the church, now that I am out of it. From the inside of the church all true and accurate information about the Mormon Church is seen as being anti-Mormon. From the inside looking out, it seemed that for some strange reason people appeared to be opposed to Mormons. In the twisted way of thinking when you are inside a cult, reality is turned upside down and what should make rational sense does not. I did not realize that I was so dominated by a spirit of fear, that I would not read any information that "appeared" to be opposed to the church. There is plenty of accurate information available about the truth of Mormonism, but if someone had tried to share it with me before I was un-blinded, I would not have seen it for what it really was.

Widespread use of the internet today has caused quite a few Mormons to find the real truth about the Mormon Church, especially its history. The church was responsible for the death of innocent men, women, and children in the Mountain Meadows Massacre, even though it would deny this reality[16]. The church functions more like a political organization than a church. Inside the church there is very little freedom. Where you live determines where you go to church. The last time I was attending a ward, I attempted to attend church with my sister, and was told by my Bishop that for me to go to church with my sister I would need the approval of the "First Presidency" in Salt Lake City, Utah. This sounds ridiculous to someone who actually has freedom in worship. Everything in the Mormon Church is organized from the top to the bottom. The corporation of the Church is run by a prophet, his two counselors, and twelve apostles. The church is organized somewhat like an army. Members actually have an opportunity to "sustain" their leaders by raising their hands in support of them. Over my many years in the church, I never saw anyone vote against a person being called to any position. There was always unanimous support of all the leaders, from the general authorities in Utah down to the local leaders on a ward or stake level. As a faithful Mormon, a person is expected to sustain his or her leaders in full obedience. To not follow a leader is to not follow God.

Little did I know that what I was doing in Mormon temples for twenty-six years was very similar to what Masons do in their "secret" ceremonies. Joseph Smith became a Mason in Nauvoo, Illinois[17]. This is how he was influenced to create a Mormon temple ceremony. He developed a "family - Celestial" version of Masonry, one that brought the entire family unit under its control. Symbolism used in Mormon temples is very similar to the symbolism found in Masonry[18].

Reading a book about masonry actually helped me to see what Mormonism really was. As I read about what masons do in their ceremonies, I recognized signs, tokens, and language that were almost the same as what I was familiar with in Mormon temple ceremonies.

August 3, 2009

2 Peter 1: 19-21   And so we have the prophetic word confirmed, which you do well to heed as a light that shines in a dark place, until the day dawns and the morning star rises in your hearts; knowing this first, that no prophecy of Scripture is of any private interpretation, for prophecy never came by the will of man, but holy men of God spoke as they were moved by the Holy Spirit.

God brought me out of the darkness and un-blinded my eyes on April 12, 2009. The night before, after reading the New Testament for a year, I finally had the courage to ask God to let me know if the Mormon Church was not true. The next morning, Easter Sunday, the veil was removed from my eyes. In many ways, it was the best day of my life but was also heart wrenching as I could now see how deceived I had been. I had done the unthinkable. I had raised my three precious children in a cult. I had given well over half my life to a godless organization organized by man. I realized in one day that Joseph Smith was not a true prophet. The church was not true. The covenants I had made were not with God. The priesthood possessed no divine authority to act in God's name on the earth. My family had never been sealed together for time and eternity. The kingdom of God had not been restored to the earth. It was all a big lie. In one day everything that had been white became black and everything that was black became white. My whole world turned upside down, at least that is how it felt.

I have been collecting old books for years. About ten years ago I came across an old book that was titled <u>Polygamy – or the Mysteries and Crimes of Mormonism</u>. I bought it because I thought it was anti-Mormon, and I wanted to take it out of circulation. It is actually true Mormon history and was written by a man named J.H. Beadle who had been an editor for the Salt Lake Reporter newspaper, as well as a clerk for the Supreme Court of Utah in the 1800's.[19] He dedicated the book to "the women of America, whose sympathies are ever active in behalf of their suffering and oppressed sisters," he proceeded to write… "This volume is respectfully dedicated to these women…in the hope that it will interest them in the condition of the women who are living in moral bondage in Utah.[20]" He wrote this book based on various writings of Mormons themselves, personal records of people who spent many years among Mormons, evidence published by the State of Missouri, as well as other official documents of states or "General government." On page nine of this book the author quotes from an article written by Louis N. Megaree, published in his weekly magazine called *Seen and Heard*. Speaking of a newspaper published in Nauvoo called the *Expositor*, Mr. Megaree quotes the *Expositor* – "In its first number they printed the affidavits of sixteen women to the effect that Smith (Joseph Smith), Rigdon (Sidney Rigdon), and others had endeavored to convert them to the spiritual wife doctrine (polygamy) and seduce them from their husbands on the plea of special revelation from heaven." Joseph Smith, along with others burned this Expositor newspaper office to the ground.[21]

August 4, 2009

Psalm 120: 1   In my distress I cried to the Lord, and He heard me.

Joseph Smith had absolutely no regard for the sanctity of marriage. I learned from reading the Tanner's book that an early church leader named Oliver Cowdery accused Joseph Smith of committing adultery in 1837 with a woman named Fanny Alger.[22] It was later recorded by Andrew Jensen, who was an assistant L.D.S. historian, that Fanny Alger was one of the "first plural wives sealed to the prophet".[23] There is even evidence from the LDS Doctrine and Covenants, that Joseph Smith was already practicing plural marriage before he claimed to "inquire of the Lord" to see if it was right.[24] It is stated even today in Section 132 of the Doctrine and Covenants (one of four books of Mormon Scripture), that plural marriage is justifiable in God's sight.[25] Even the practice of taking concubines is seen as honorable. "Abraham received concubines, and they bore him children; and it was accounted unto him for righteousness" is how it is written.[26] The author Fawn Brodie in her book entitled No Man Knows my History, lists 48 women who may have been married to Joseph Smith.[27] Through temple work for the dead, it is supposed that Joseph Smith was "sealed in eternal marriage" to 246 women.[28] According to Mormon doctrine, it is believed that Joseph Smith will have all these women as his wives in eternity.

Joseph Smith took other men's wives while he was alive. He taught that all previous marriage covenants were done away with, and that none were binding but the new covenants that he himself was performing.[29] In a sermon delivered in the Salt Lake Tabernacle in 1854 by Jedediah M. Grant, second counselor to Brigham Young, he stated "what would a man of God say, who felt aright, when Joseph asked him for his money? He would say, "Yes, and I wish I had more help to build up the kingdom of God! or if he came and said, 'I want your wife, O yes he would say, Here she is, there are plenty more.'[30] One of the early Mormon apostles, Heber C. Kimball, in responding to "the Lord's command" for him to give his wife to Joseph Smith, apologized to Joseph because his wife would not comply, and instead both Heber C. Kimball and his wife offered Joseph Smith their adolescent daughter. They gave their daughter named Helen Mar to Joseph Smith as one of his wives.[31] Joseph Smith took one man's wife while that man was out of town.[32] Author Juanita Brooks wrote "Joseph not only paid his addresses to the young and unmarried women, but he sought 'spiritual' alliances with many married ladies...he taught them that all former marriages were null and void, and that they were at perfect liberty to make another choice of a husband. The marriage covenants were not binding, because they were ratified only by Gentile laws. These laws 'the Lord' did not recognize; consequently all the women were free. One woman said to me not very long since, while giving me some of her experiences in polygamy: 'The greatest trial I ever endured in my life was living with my husband and deceiving him, by receiving Joseph's attention whenever he chose to come to me. These women, and others, whose experience had been very similar, are among the very best women in the church; they are as pure minded and virtuous women as any in the world. They were seduced under the guise of religion...some of these women have since said they did not know who was the father of their children; this is not to be wondered at, for promiscuity was practiced; and, indeed, all sense of morality seemed to have been lost by a portion at least of the church.[33]"

Sarah Pratt, the wife of the Apostle Orson Pratt, was sought by Joseph Smith while her husband was away in Europe serving a mission for the church. In his book, published in 1842, entitled <u>History of the Saints</u>, John C.

Bennett stated that "Joe Smith told me, confidentially, during the absence of her husband, that he intended to make Mrs. Pratt as one of his spiritual wives...for the Lord had given her to him as a special favor for his faithfulness and zeal. He then went to her house and told her about these things and threatened her reputation if she refused him.[34]"

"For many years before coming up with a marriage or sealing ceremony, Joseph Smith stated to his intended victims... 'God does not care if we have a good time, if only other people do not know it!' He only introduced a marriage ceremony when he had found out that he could not get certain women without it."[35] One woman, Nancy Rigdon, a daughter of church leader Sidney Rigdon, was sought by Joseph Smith, and he offered his friend John C. Bennett five hundred dollars, or the best lot on Main Street to help him get her as his wife. Joseph Smith's plot was to approach Miss Rigdon, in the name of the Lord, by special revelation. This he did. He took her into a private room and locked the door...Then swore her to secrecy and told her that she had long been the idol of his affections, and that he had asked the Lord for her, and that it was his holy will that he should have her.[36] She refused him. Joseph Smith though wrote a letter to her in which he stated that "Happiness is the object and design of our existence ...that which is wrong under one circumstance, may be, and often is, right under another.[37]" Joseph Smith married five pairs of sisters and even a mother and daughter, Patty and Sylvia Sessions.[38] He even had his own sister sealed to him for eternity.[39] One revelation given by Joseph Smith regarding polygamy is reportedly preserved in a vault in the LDS church Historical Department. Although the church has a policy of suppressing important records, Sandra and Gerald Tanner were able to examine a microfilm of this revelation in 1976. This revelation is obviously controversial in that it commanded Mormons to marry Indians, to make them a "white" and "delightsome" people.[40]

Joseph Lee Robinson, a Mormon polygamist himself, once made the comment that "plural marriage...is calculated in its nature to severely try the women even to nearly tear their heart strings out of them.[41]. Mormon leaders actually taught that a woman was inferior, and that her salvation depended on a man.[42] One woman raised in a polygamist family, Daisy Barclay, commented "Polygamy is predicated on the assumption that a man is superior to a woman..." Mormon tradition follows that of the ancient Hebrews. It teaches a woman to honor and obey her husband, and look upon him as her Lord and Master. In referring to her mother she stated "Mother figures you are supposed to spend your life taking care of a man, and he is God.[43]" Brigham Young, second prophet of the Mormon Church said in one of his sermons, "The man is the head and God of the woman, but let him act like a God in virtuous principles.[44]"

The revelation on polygamy in section 132 of the Doctrine and Covenants, contradicts Section 58 of the Doctrine and Covenants, in that section 58 states that a person "that keeps the laws of God has no need to break the laws of the land. In practicing polygamy in Illinois, the Mormons did violate the state laws against bigamy. Even though the Mormon Church leaders knew that polygamy was a crime, they considered themselves and those that followed them to be above the law. Brigham Young once commented, "If I had forty wives in the United States, they did not know it, and could not substantiate it, neither did I ask any lawyer, judge, or magistrate for them, I live above the law, and so do this people.[45]"

Wicked deeds are done by vile and wicked men. Sometimes they deceive others to follow them in their wickedness. Joseph Smith and the men that surrounded him have caused many hearts to be deceived and ultimately broken. They will answer to God for it.

August 6, 2009

Psalm 124: 7 Our soul has escaped as a bird from the snare of the fowlers; the snare is broken, and we have escaped.

As Joseph Smith was not a prophet inspired by God, it is not difficult to determine who he was directed by. He was demonically directed. The real story of how the Book of Mormon came to be is much different from the whitewashed tale that is taught inside the Mormon Church. The story they tell is about a guileless young boy of fourteen who sought God in prayer in a grove of trees in upper state New York, because he did not know which church to join. The church deceptively teaches potential converts, as well as members, that Joseph Smith was a chosen vessel of God to "restore" the true church to the earth. They teach that he was visited by an angel named Moroni, who led him to some gold plates that had been buried by a prophet from an ancient civilization of people called the Nephites and the Lamanites, who were supposedly of Jewish ancestry. The Church teaches that he translated these plates by God's power, and published his manuscript as the Book of Mormon.

The true story is very different. I also learned by reading the Tanner's book, that the true story of how the Book of Mormon came to be is a story of darkness and magical practice. There seemed to have been a certain "religious delusion" that was occurring in an area of Vermont around

1800. A man by the name of Nathaniel Woods saw himself and his followers as modern Jews or Israelites and claimed that he was being led by God. In the *Vermont Historical Gazette*, it is recorded that the Woods movement gave rise to the Mormon movement. Joseph Smith's father, Joseph Smith Sr. was said to have been one of the leading "rodsmen" in the Woods movement. The followers of Nathaniel Wood used a hazel rod (from a witch hazel bush) as a medium for revelation. Nathaniel Wood was referred to as "Priest Wood". The hazel rod was used to tell if someone was sick, whether he or she would die or not, as well as for all their business matters. It was said that the Woods were "very fruitful in prophecies," especially after they began using these hazel rods. The first man in this movement to use the hazel-rod was a "fugitive from justice", a counterfeiter named Winchell, who searched along with Joseph Smith Sr. for money or buried treasure in the hills and mountains around Palmyra, New York.[46]

Governor Ford of Illinois wrote of the young Joseph Smith, Jr. "his extreme youth was spent in an idle, vagabond life, roaming in the woods, dreaming of buried treasures, and exerting the art of finding them by twisting a forked stick in his hands...He and his father before him, were what are called 'water witches'. Joseph Smith's father used the hazel-rod to 'obtain revelations' and young Joseph Smith was taught to do the same.[47] In 1834, E.D. Howe published statements and affidavits of people who knew Joseph Smith and his family. One man, Joshua Stafford, who had come to know the Smith family around 1820, said they were a poor family who started digging for hidden treasures in order to make money. It was said that they became "indolent" and told "marvelous stories about ghosts, hobgoblins, caverns, and various other mysterious matters." Another man, Joseph

Capron, said that the Smith family held their son, Joseph Smith Jr. "in high estimation on account of some supernatural power which he was supposed to possess.⁴⁸" Joseph Smith, Jr. was arrested, tried, and found guilty by a justice of the peace in Bainbridge, New York in 1826. He was charged with misdemeanor vagrancy while living with a man named Josiah Stowel. Josiah Stowel had come to Joseph Smith for help in finding hidden treasure. He came to Joseph Smith because he had heard that Smith "possessed certain keys" to be able to "discern things invisible to the natural eye." Smith was becoming known as a man having a gift of "seership". In the court document of 1826, Joseph Smith is referred to as a "glasslooker". This is because he had begun using a stone that had been found in 1822, while he was helping a man named Willard Chase to dig a well. A man named William D. Purple wrote an account of the Bainbridge trial. He wrote that Josiah Stowel had heard about Joseph Smith "who, by the aid of a magic stone had become a famous seer of lost or hidden treasures," and that "by means of the stone which he placed in his hat, and by excluding the light from all other terrestrial things, could see whatever he wished, even in the depths of the earth. During this trial a man named Mr. Thompson who worked for Josiah Stowel, testified the following: Smith had told Josiah Stowel that "very many years before a band of robbers had buried on his flat a box of treasure, and as it was very valuable they had by a sacrifice placed a charm over it to protect it, so that it could not be obtained except by faith, accompanied by certain talismanic influences. So, after arming themselves with fasting and prayer, they sallied forth to the spot designated by Smith. Digging was commenced with fear and trembling, in the presence of this imaginary charm. In a few feet from the surface the box of treasure was struck by the shovel, on which they redoubled their energies, but it gradually receded from their grasp. One of the men placed his hand upon the box, but it gradually sunk from his reach...Mr. Stowel went to his flock, and selected a fine vigorous lamb, and resolved to sacrifice it to the demon spirit who guarded the coveted treasure. Shortly after the venerable Deacon (Mr. Stowel) might be seen on his knees at prayer near the pit, while Smith, with a lantern in one hand to dispel the midnight darkness might be seen making a circuit around the spot, sprinkling the flowing blood from the lamb upon the ground, as a propitiation to the spirit that thwarted them. They then descended the excavation, but the treasure still receded from their grasp, and it was never obtained. This took place about four years before Joseph Smith claimed to find the "Gold Bible."[49] A man named William Stafford had the following dealing with Joseph Smith and Joseph Smith's father: "Joseph Smith, Sen., came to me one night, and told me, that Joseph Smith Jr. had been looking in his glass, and had seen, not many rods from his house, two or three kegs of gold and silver, some feet under the surface of the earth; and that none others but the elder Joseph and myself could get them. I accordingly consented to go, and early in the evening repaired to the place of deposit. Joseph Sen., first made a circle, twelve or fourteen feet in diameter. This circle, said he, contains the treasure. He then stuck in the ground a row of witch hazel sticks, around the said circle, for the purpose of keeping off the evil spirits. Within this circle he made another, of about eight or ten feet in diameter. He walked around three times on the periphery of this last circle, muttering to himself something which I could not understand. He next stuck a steel rod in the centre of the circles, and then enjoined profound silence upon us, lest we should arouse the evil spirit who had the charge of these treasures. After we had dug a trench about five feet in depth around the rod, the old man by signs and motions, asked leave of absence, and went to the house to inquire of young Joseph the cause of our disappointment. He soon returned and said, that Joseph had remained all this time in the house, looking in his stone and watching the motions of the evil spirit – that he saw the spirit come up to the ring and as soon as it beheld the cone which we had formed around the rod, it caused the money to sink. We then went into the house, and the old man observed, that we had made a mistake in the commencement of the operation; if it had not been for that, said he, we should have got the money...Old Joseph and one of the boys came to me one day, and said that Joseph Jr. had discovered some very remarkable and valuable treasures, which could be procured only in one way. That way, was as follows: - That a black sheep should be taken on to the ground where the treasures were concealed – that after cutting its throat, it should be led around a circle while bleeding. This being done, the wrath of the evil spirit would be appeased: the treasures could then be obtained, and my share of them was to be fourfold. To gratify my curiosity, I let them have a large fat sheep. They afterwards informed me, that the sheep was killed pursuant to commandment; but as there was some mistake in the process, it did not have the desired effect. This, I believe, is the only time they ever made money-digging a profitable business...when they found that the people of this vicinity would no longer put any faith in their schemes for digging money; then they pretended to find a gold bible...[50]" Joseph Capron came to know Joseph Smith, Sr. in 1827. He told of Joseph Smith, Jr. by using his seer stone was able to see "anything he wished". Through this stone Joseph Smith, Jr. discovered "ghosts, infernal spirits, mountains of gold and silver, and many other invaluable treasures deposited in the earth". Joseph claimed to have discovered a chest of gold watches just northwest of Joseph Capron's house. Smith claimed though that "as they were in the possession of the evil spirit, it required skill and stratagem to obtain them." He then gave Mr. Capron orders to "stick a parcel of large stakes in the ground, several rods around, in a circular form. This was to be done directly over the spot where the treasures were deposited." Smith then sent a messenger to Palmyra to obtain a polished sword in his hand, marched around to guard any assault which his satanic majesty might be disposed to make." In the end, "the devil came off victorious, and carried away the watches." Mr. Capron then mentions that "at length, Joseph pretended to find the Gold plates" which scheme was thought to enable the Smith family to make a profit.[51]"

It seems the idea about finding a book came to Joseph Smith from a man named Walters who was referred to as "the conjurer." Walters used a book of Cicero's Orations, written in Latin that he pretended to interpret for people. He claimed that this book was a record of the former inhabitants of America.[52] Isaac Butts attended school with Joseph Smith, Jr. He said Joseph Smith had a forked witch-hazel rod which he claimed he could find buried treasure with, as well as a peep stone that he also used .[53] A Mrs. S.F. Anderick said that Joseph Smith deceived many farmers into digging at night for chests of gold. When the pick struck a chest and someone spoke out loud, Smith would claim the enchantment had been broken and the chest would leave.[54]. C.M. Stafford stated that "Jo claimed to have revelations and tell fortunes...Jo had men dig on a tunnel forty or fifty feet long in a hill about two miles north of where he claimed to find the plates. I have been in it.[55]" David Whitmer, one of the three "witnesses" to the Book of Mormon, admitted that Joseph Smith placed a seer stone into a hat to translate the Book of Mormon. "Joseph Smith did not see the plates in translation, but would hold the interpreters (Urim and

Thummim) to his eyes and cover his face with a hat, excluding all light, and before him would appear what seemed to be parchment on which would appear the characters of the plates on a line at the top, and immediately below would appear the translation in English,...[56]" Emma, Joseph Smith's wife, and Joseph Smith's mother, both stated that the plates were on a table while Josesph "translated" them with his eyes hid in a hat with a seer stone.[57] There were also many early Mormons who had their own peep stones with which they claimed to be able to receive revelations. [58] Although most Mormons are taught that Joseph Smith translated the gold plates by using a "urim and thummim", a former prophet of the church, Joseph Fielding Smith stated that the urim and thummim was actually the seer stone that Joseph Smith had in the early days of the church.[59] Even the Mormon apostle Bruce R. McConkie stated in his book, <u>Mormon Doctrine</u>, that "in imitation of the true order of heaven whereby seers receive revelations from God through a urim and thummim, the devil gives his own revelations to some of his followers through peep stones or crystal balls.[60] Interestingly enough, years later in 1888 on May 17th, LDS prophet Wilford Woodruff, in a private dedication service in the Manti Utah temple "consecrated upon the altar the seer stone that Joseph Smith found by revelation some thirty feet under the earth, and (subsequently) carried with him throughout life.[61]" As recent as 1971, Joseph Anderson, assistant to the Council of twelve apostles, told Dean Hooper of Rockford, Illinois at a Chicago Stake Conference that "the seer stone that Joseph Smith used in the early days of the church, is in the possession of the church, and is kept in a safe in (then prophet) Joseph Fielding Smith's office." Anderson said he had seen it there "a number of times."[62] One would wonder if a stone kept in a safe in the prophet's office which had been seen "a number of times" is not still in use today by the current prophet, Thomas S. Monson? Since the Mormon Church claims to be continuing to receive revelation, it would make sense that it is still done today the same way it was done by Joseph Smith.

August 10, 2009

Psalm 126: 6 He who continually goes forth weeping, bearing seed for sowing, shall doubtless come again with rejoicing, bringing his sheaves with him.

Truly as for any strength of my own, I am nothing. The Lord holds me. Satan would whisper lies to me that I have taken the lonely, hard road, where I am all alone. That is not true. God is with me, and I know if He is with me, that Satan cannot overcome me. Satan tries to lie to me and tell me that I have left the familiar shore where I had some false guarantee that my family would be together forever IF we satisfied the never-satisfied god of Mormonism. I have left the familiar shore, and can now see it more clearly for what it was – a delusion. It was a delusion that everything was somehow okay within "the kingdom of God." Although I may be far away from what was familiar to me, I know God has been with me, and is with me every step of the way. My husband has been a rock to me. He has been a great blessing to me. I know that if I am doing God's will, that He will sustain me, and I am learning that even if I mess up, he will not be waiting with a brutal sword of justice to bring me back in line. I am learning about grace. It truly is amazing! Some days are easier than others. I still often feel like I am in some kind of fog, but slowly I am learning to let go and to trust. Before that day this past April, when everything went from white to black and black to white, I drove to the local LDS chapel late one night and cried, because up until that time it had seemed that the church had been the safest place in my life (even with my doubts about it). I had associated from age nine many fond memories with the church. When our neighbors in Lubbock took my sister and me to church with them for children's activities during the week it seemed like such a safe and happy place to be. At that time, how little did I know, years later I would come to understand the painful truth about what the church actually was. Now, so many memories, people, pictures, places, events in my past are tainted with the dark truth about Mormonism. I do not know how I could make it day by day without the support of my husband, as well as other Christian people we are around. We also have two grandsons that bring great joy into our lives. They have all become like a living lifeline to me, as so often I feel like I am a ship all alone lost out at sea. The Christian brothers and sisters at the church we are going to are like angels to me. Even though I do not tell people much about how I am feeling, their kindness has helped to sustain me. I know that I am out of the storm, or so it seems, but now the emotional fallout is sweeping over me. How grateful I am to know that God is at the helm and I am not.

August 11, 2009

Psalm 124 "If it had not been the Lord who was on our side," Let Israel now say; "If it had not been the Lord who was on our side, when men rose up against us, then they would have swallowed us alive, when their wrath was kindled against us; then the waters would have overwhelmed us, the stream would have gone over our soul." Then the swollen waters would have gone over our soul." Blessed be the Lord, who has not given us as prey to their teeth. Our soul has escaped as a bird from the snare of the fowlers; the snare is broken, and we have escaped.

Our help is in the name of the Lord, Who made heaven and earth.

I could not write any words today, they just would not come.

August 14, 2009

Psalm 136: 1   Oh, give thanks to the Lord, for He is good! For His mercy endures forever.

Psalm 136: 16 To Him who led His people through the wilderness, for His mercy endures forever.

Truly God's mercy endures forever! He has led me through my wilderness. As my heart is healing and I am coming to know more about God and about His amazing grace, I look back and see His hand in our lives. I actually looked at old family pictures today, and can see that God blessed me with many good times. Only God can heal us. He can take our pathetic, broken, bruised selves and bear us up. He can bring light to the darkest of times, and the most frightening places. It is all about Him, not about us. We are nothing. He is everything. We are weak. He is strong. We are failing. He is faithful.

August 17, 2009

Psalm 42: 5   Why are you cast down, O my soul? And why are you disquieted within me? Hope in God, for I shall yet praise Him for the help of His countenance.

My God is with me. Today is my 46th birthday, and my God is with me. How abundant is His grace and glorious is His mercy. He has brought me home. He has given my heart hope. He has opened new paths for me to follow. I am learning more about the church my husband and I are attending. He has been a member there for about ten years. I started going there in May of 2008. It was so different from what I was accustomed to in the Mormon Church. It felt so free. It has taken me about a year and three months now to really feel comfortable there. Because the Mormon Church is so structured and hierarchal (dictatorial) in its administration, I was accustomed to being "called" to serve in the church. At the church I am at now (Dallas Bay Baptist Church in Hixson, Tennessee), individuals can allow the Spirit of God to lead them where and how they serve. People are encouraged to be real at Dallas Bay. This is so refreshing after where I have come from. This has been so healing. God has given me a place to learn to trust Him more, and know Him better. I have never felt judged at Dallas Bay, and that has brought me much courage and strength.

Leaving Mormonism and coming into an evangelical church, is like going from living in Communist China to living in a free country. It has been a cultural change. There were new words being used that I did not understand. People were using certain terms like "grace", "saved", and "legalism", which I did not understand. Slowly it became easier.

August 20, 2009

Psalm 139: 7-13 Where can I go from Your Spirit? Or where can I flee from Your presence? If I ascend into heaven, You are there: if I make my bed in hell, behold, You are there. If I take the wings of the morning, and dwell in the uttermost parts of the sea, even there Your hand shall lead me, and Your right hand shall hold me. If I say, "Surely the darkness shall fall on me," even the night shall be light about me; indeed, the darkness shall not hide from You, but the night shines as the day; the darkness and the light are both alike to You. For You formed my inward parts; you covered me in my mother's womb.

After emerging from my blindness, God helped me put one foot in front of the other. My initial reaction was to run away from anything and everything that reminded me of Mormonism. From words I would hear pastors speak, to seeing Boy Scouts camping in a campground, so many things reminded me of my time as a Mormon. Slowly this got better, but it was a daily struggle. I knew that God wanted me to continue to go to church, and to take seminary classes with my husband, so I did so. My heart, though, really wanted to run away from anything that reminded me of my time as a Mormon. That is one of Satan's tricks when a person realizes the truth about the Mormon church. He or she will often stay away from all churches, because of the pain and betrayal they feel.

After my blindness was lifted, I struggled with emotions and feelings that I had left so many people that I cared about behind. I felt tremendous guilt that God had rescued me, and not others that I love. I have had many nightmares since my blindness was lifted, where so many I love are still trapped. In these nightmares I am always trying to reach them and lead them to safety, but I cannot.

August 21, 2009

Psalm 141: 7-8 Our bones are scattered at the mouth of the grave, as when one plows and breaks up the earth. But my eyes are upon You, O God the Lord; in You I take refuge; do not leave my soul destitute.

I know and understand now that the place of our greatest pain is the place of our greatest freedom. It is the place where God will do His best work, if we allow Him to do so. He is there waiting for us. God calls us into our sorrows. The places of our greatest fears may with God, become landmarks of His grace and courage. His arm is never too short to reach us. He is always there as the compassionate healer of our hearts. The road He has called me to walk down has become one where He is continually showing Himself strong, as the reality of the situation frightens and disturbs me at times. He however, has been down all the roads of our lives as He knows the end from the beginning. He is our only source of hope and truth. As my situation has become darker, God has given me more light. As I have become broken down to nothing, God has become so much greater and stronger to me.

September 6, 2009

Psalm 1: 1-3 Blessed is the man who walks not in the counsel of the ungodly, nor stands in the path of sinners, nor sits in the seat of the scornful; but his delight is in the law of the Lord, and in His law he meditates day and night. He shall be like a tree planted by the rivers of water, that brings forth its fruit in its season, whose leaf also shall not wither; and whatsoever he does shall prosper.

God is at work all around us. The more my heart opens, the more I can see this. God is not in the storm, God uses the storm. I cannot blame God in any way for the storms of my life, but I can lay this broken heart down at His feet, and allow Him to use the storms of my life to most fully glorify Him. He redeems and restores. He takes that which is broken, and puts it back together in the way that glorifies Him.

The storms of my life have disoriented me. They have caused me confusion and heartache. So many things I went through in my blindness, I never grieved the way I should have. I realize now, more than ever, only in God is there security. So much can change and shift in our lives. People die, relationships change, jobs are lost, houses become empty and what remains? God remains. All goes away, or may go away and change, except God. In the end, as Solomon discovered, nothing satisfies except God. Nothing endures except God. Yesterday is over and gone, but God remains. This world's parties and celebrations end, but God remains. The seasons of our lives come and go, but God remains.

September 7, 2009

Psalm 5: 8-12   Lead me, O Lord, in Your righteousness because of my enemies; make Your way straight before my face. For there is no faithfulness in their mouth; their inward part is destruction; their inward part is destruction; their throat is an open tomb; they flatter with their tongue. Pronounce them guilty, O God! Let them fall by their own counsels; Cast them out in the multitude of their transgressions; for they have rebelled against You. But let all those rejoice who put their trust in You; let them ever shout for joy, because You defend them; let those also who love Your name be joyful in You. For You, O Lord, will bless the righteous; with favor You will surround him as with a shield.

God's grace has been at work throughout my life, although I did not understand it at the time. God's hand is present in our lives even when we through ignorance, disobedience, or foolishness do not see it.

One of the most evil designs of Mormon doctrine is the doctrine relating to the family. The Mormon priesthood claims the power and authority to seal families together for eternity. This is, of course, based on the faithfulness of the individual to the teachings of the church. So for someone like me who was sealed to my family, my leaving the church was seen as leaving my family.

The only eternal family any of us will ever be in is God's family. We only become part of His family by accepting what His Son did for us on the cross. He paid the price for us to be part of His family forever. The only hope I have for my family is that they will become part of God's family by accepting the free gift of grace through Jesus Christ. Only through Christ alone is there any hope of family relationships continuing after this life.

September 8, 2009

1 Samuel 17: 45-47 Then David said to the Philistine, "You come to me with a sword, with a spear, and with a javelin. But I come to you in the name of the Lord of Hosts, the God of the armies of Israel, whom you have defied." "This day the Lord will deliver you into my hand, and I will strike you, and take your head from you. And this day I will give the carcasses of the camp of the Philistines to the birds of the air and the wild beasts of the earth, that all the earth may know that there is a God in Israel." "Then all this assembly shall know that the Lord does not save with sword and spear; for the battle is the Lord's, and He will give you into our hands."

The battle is the Lord's. It is not mine. I cannot fix what is broken in my life. I know without a doubt that the times throughout my life when I leaned on the Lord (even in my blindness), that He held me up. He directed me. He gave me comfort. He sustained me. When I read the words of the Bible, and put my faith in His words, He guided me with His words. He was my light and my lifeline; although seemingly faint during my blindness at least that is how it seemed.

The truth still stings, but now I see. His will has taken me far away from everything that is familiar to me, but I know that He goes before us when He leads us to places we don't understand.

September 16, 2009

1 Samuel 28: 16-19 Then Samuel said: "So why do you ask me, seeing the Lord has departed from you, and has become your enemy? "And the Lord has done for Himself, as he spoke by me. For the Lord hath torn the kingdom out of your hand and given it to your neighbor, David. "Because you did not obey the voice of the Lord, nor execute His fierce wrath upon Amalek, therefore the Lord has done this thing to you this day. "Moreover the Lord will also deliver Israel with you into the hand of the Philistines. And tomorrow you and your sons will be with me. The Lord will also deliver the army of Israel into the hand of the Philistines."

All works of darkness will one day end, and all the enemies of God will come to nothing. They will fall into the traps that they have laid for others. Their evil, vile works will be turned upon their own heads, and their judgment will come from the hand of God. Those people, who now take pleasure and satisfaction in deceiving and harming others, will meet their just reward. They may obtain temporary benefit for a season in Satan's kingdom, but in the end, they too will fall along with his kingdom. Satan's kingdom has an expiration date.

God's kingdom is the one that will go on forever and ever. Every knee will bow and every tongue confess one day to the one and only true God, Jesus Christ the Lord of heaven and earth.

From Joseph Smith to the current leaders of the Mormon Church today, *John 8: 44* applies to them; *"You are of your father the devil, and the desires of your father you want to do. He was a murderer from the beginning, and does not stand in the truth, because there is no truth in him. When he speaks a lie, he speaks from his own resources, for he is a liar, and the father of it."*

They are deceiving people. Their works are not of God, but of the father of lies. As it says in *2 Cor. 11: 13-14 "For such are false apostles, deceitful workers, transforming themselves into apostles of Christ. And no wonder! For Satan himself transforms himself into an angel of light."* This can be said of the leaders of the Mormon Church. Joseph Smith was a false prophet who was directed by the forces of darkness to proclaim and publish "another" gospel. The Book of Mormon was brought about through demonic influence. It may contain some sprinklings of truth from the Bible, but these are only there to entice people into believing the lies that it contains. Joseph Smith arrogantly claimed to establish his own translation of the Bible. He did what is spoken of in *Galatians 1: 6-9, "I marvel that you are turning away so soon from Him who called you in the grace of Christ, to a different gospel, which is not another; but there are some who trouble you and want to pervert the gospel of Christ. But even if we, or an angel from heaven, preach any other gospel to you than what we have preached to you, let him be accursed..."* Joseph Smith, as well as many Mormons today, and for many years have preached "another" gospel.

109

It is so tragic that so many Mormons actually think that they are Christians. They do not know the Jesus Christ of the Bible. They do not understand who His is. Their church leaders tell them they are Christians, and they often have no clue how they have been deceived into believing "another gospel". Most Mormons I knew had no understanding of what true Christianity was all about. I did not understand the Bible as a Mormon. Inside the church, a person is carefully kept away from the liberating teachings of grace. The way the church functions, intentionally keeps peoples' attention turned to its false doctrine, and ultimately led astray and blinded by it.

Grace is a foreign concept to a Mormon. It was a foreign concept to me. I would hear the words to the song "*Amazing Grace,*" and I would wonder what people were singing about. It was a nice song and I liked it, but I had no understanding of what it meant. I had been led to believe "another gospel" of works, ultimately worshipping another god who was not a god of grace. What happened to the Galatians, happened to me. I was a born again Christian who was "bewitched" by another gospel. I was led astray, very far astray. In my ignorance I led others astray.

Any new Christian who knows very little about who God is or about His Word, as well as any not so new Christian who does not study the simple doctrines of the Bible are prime candidates for deception. They are vulnerable to teachers of false doctrine. False teachers are all around us, and have been since the inception of the church. How critical it is to know God's Word. If one thinks that they cannot be blinded they are wrong. If they do not "show themselves approved" and become ready to give a defense for the hope that lies within them, they can be led to believe lies. What an amazing thing it is that we have God's Word to read and study. How many believers there have been over many centuries who would have loved to live in our day, especially under the freedoms we now enjoy as Americans and be able to have such abundant access to God's Word! Satan does not want people to be able to study or know God's Word. For years the Catholic Church did not want their members to have access to the Bible. Atheistic, communist countries attempt to abolish the Word of God. Cults pervert the Word of God, and interpret it incorrectly. I believe God will hold us accountable for how we have used His word. If we have had access to it, and have not taken the time to learn and study it, the day may come when we truly regret this.

The following entries are some psalms I wrote.

October 17, 2009

O God my Shelter. You are strong thru storm and rain, as soft places become hard, and day turns into night, Your name remains. O God my strength, You are my only foundation, as pleasures turn to pain, and warm memories turn to dust, You are there. O God my light, you alone have become my eyes, as visions of beauty die, and promises fall to the ground, you bring again the sunshine. O God my all, beside you there is none, as those who called me by name call me no longer, as safe places are safe no more, you bring me to you and are my only safe place.

October 21, 2009

God has brought me to a new place. He has seen fit to bring me into His everlasting light. He has taken away blindness from my eyes. He has brought me to Himself. Now I belong to Him and no other. He has bought me with His precious blood. I belong to this dying world no longer. All my ways have been known to Him and to no other. His promises have dwelt in my heart like drops of rain on desert sand. His words have rested in my soul as crumbs of bread give life to a dying sparrow. His arm has carried me through dark tunnels of terror where death lay around me. His hand closed upon mine in gentleness when ravenous wolves made me their home. He heard my every cry, and spoke to me words of life.

God is God forever, though all around us moves, and earth grows older still, and daytime gives way to night; God is God forever, though rulers rise and fall, and knowledge of man comes to nothing, and the world's wisdom fails; God is God forever, though the evil day increases, and storms rage in men's hearts, and nothing is as it seems; God is God forever, though great mountains of our lives crumble, and living leaves us dying, and our hearts are torn from us; God is God forever.

October 28, 2009

Places of refuge have become places of death, all light became dark, happiness faded away, and God was revealed, false foundations fled away, smiles hid swords, all that once held tight broke, warmth turned cold, and God was there. Names familiar were forgotten, talk became silence, all embraces fell still, familiar became foreign, and God stood firm.

CHAPTER 6

THE POWER OF A HYMN

The words of this old hymn helped me for many years to know that there was a firm foundation somewhere, even though I was not on it...

How firm a foundation, ye saints of the Lord,
Is laid for your faith in His excellent word!
What more can he say, than to you he hath said,
You, who unto Jesus for refuge hath fled.

Where is our peace? Ultimately, the right question and the only question regarding our peace is – Who is our peace? Everything in life changes – except God. Outside of Him, there is no peace. For so many years in my blindness, the words of this old hymn gave my heart rest. It helped me to know a little more about who God was, and how I could trust Him when there was so much about my life I did not understand. It was never the Mormon Church that brought peace, it was the trickles of understanding I gathered from the words of this hymn, along with the Word of God that I read in the Bible that brought me comfort, even though my understanding and interpretation of God's word was so faulty. It was like the truths about God were highlighted by God, even though I was in the midst of so much false teaching.

Just over three years after meeting my husband, and two years after my eyes were miraculously opened to the truth about the deception of Mormon doctrine, I look back and see that the God that I trusted in, the God I understood a little more about by singing the above hymn, is the same God I can now trust so much more. Why is this? It is because without knowing that God has revealed Himself to us in His Word – the Bible, and realizing that in that book alone we have all we need to come to know Him better, we are not set free. It was the word of God applied through the Spirit of God which removed my blindness. It was the passion and earnestness of my husband, his love of God, his boldness, courage and faith which God used to bring me to Him.

God knows our hearts, and only He knows what we are praying and longing for. For fourteen years my prayer was "Your will God be done." I knew that God would deliver me someday (even though I did not really know what from). I knew, however, it would be in His way and in His time. If it was not for the hope and assurance God gave me, I would have not made it through.

In every condition – in sickness, in health,
In poverty's vale or abounding in wealth,
At home or abroad, on the land or the sea –
As thy days may demand, so thy succor shall be.

God continued to be good, as my family and I became more and more worn out and worn down. I put my trust in Him. I felt however, that He was far off – He loved us, but He was on His throne, and not near. I did not understand the amazing teachings of Hebrews of how we could come boldly to the throne of grace daily, and receive what we needed directly from Him. I had faith, but I did not have enough knowledge and understanding about who God was to turn to Him alone and trust Him like I should. I had been, and was being given mixed messages about Him. Some of the hymns we sung told us more about the true God, but the pagan oaths and covenants we participated in inside Mormon temples taught that God was a god of justice, not mercy. I was taught stories about Jesus, and continually told to be "Christ like", but I did not know the liberating New Testament teachings of how Christ wanted to transform us and give us a new nature, so that we could follow Him in His strength, not in our own strength.

The god Joseph Smith had worshipped was not a god that wanted to give us freedom to love, and freedom to fail – a God of grace. Joseph Smith's god did not mind breaking women's hearts as he justified taking many wives. So I lived with whispers of the true God of the Bible, but with shouts of the angry and demanding god of Mormonism. No one can worship two masters. One will eventually win out every time. Even though the angry god of Mormonism told us daily that we were not good enough (Satan is relentless and demanding when he is trying to make saints out of sinners), the true God continued to bless us in more ways than I can ever understand. We never did without. God does make His sun rise on the just, and the unjust. I did acknowledge His hand in my life, but I failed to know and trust Him as He would have wanted.

Fear not, I am with thee; oh, be not dismayed,
For I am thy God and will still give thee aid.
I'll strengthen thee, help thee, and cause thee to
stand,
Upheld by my righteous, omnipotent hand.

After our horrendous car accident in 1995, as my ex-husband was deployed to Croatia during the Bosnian war, when we struggled to make it through medical school and law school, when we were heartbroken over loved ones, when my father committed suicide, etc. we did not fear when we focused on the God spoken of in this hymn. The God described in this hymn was the One that helped us to keep going. He was omnipotent. He was big enough to understand what we were going through. Once again the small god of Mormonism, who used to be a man, was not big enough for us to trust in. We sang this hymn as a family probably hundreds of times. God somehow gets through. Even in the desert, where there is no water, and all the skies show no sign of rain, God gets through.

When our hearts were worn out and broken and we did not understand anything that was happening around us, we did not read the words of Joseph Smith – to bring us comfort. Only the amazing, all powerful God who did not want us to fear was solid and unmoving enough for us to lean on. Once more, it was not the false god "who used to be a man" that Joseph Smith taught about that we turned to for strength. It was the God of the Bible Who alone could give us rest.

When through the deep waters I call thee to go,
The rivers of sorrow shall not thee overflow,
For I will be with thee, thy troubles to bless,
And sanctify to thee thy deepest distress.

I wish I could say that all my deep waters are gone, but they are not. There have been tremendous challenges among my family members since I have come out of the Mormon church. I now openly and publicly declare that it is antichristian, anti-family, occult, and similar to Islam. The way I see it, however, I have no choice. The true God of the Bible has now become the shout, and the god of Mormonism only a faint whisper. How could I possibly not want others enslaved by Mormonism to come to know the true and living

God, the one and only God who bought and paid for us on the cross at Calvary? It is really worth any cost to be able to declare the truth of God to a lost and dying world. This has been pressed deep into my heart. My heart breaks over those who have no clue they are lost, but have been told they have been found. Mormons see themselves as followers of Jesus Christ, although they are never told in the Mormon church the simple way of salvation by grace in Christ alone. The evil nature of the false doctrines of Mormonism (darkness being taught as light) is so very disturbing. If I take the easy road and say that Mormons are okay because they believe in another "Jesus," I would be lying. It is written that even the demons believe and tremble.

When through fiery trials thy pathway shall lie,
My grace, all sufficient, shall be thy supply.
The flame shall not hurt thee; I only design
Thy dross to consume and thy gold to refine.

Now I understand a little about how true believers of Jesus Christ are persecuted. Since I was un-blinded, the Voice of the Martyrs ministry has had a special significance to me. I know that from the inception of the true church on the day of Pentecost, Christians have suffered and died for their belief in Jesus Christ. Very few people could understand this better than Paul himself. As one of the chief persecutors, he knew the hatred the Jews displayed to the new Christian believers. He knew by a life-altering, mind-focusing, heart-wrenching experience on the Damascus road just what he was doing when he was persecuting Christians. He was persecuting Jesus Christ Himself. In the years to follow, Paul would learn all too well what it felt like on the other side, as he became hated and despised for his testimony and witness of Jesus Christ.

Being disowned by those you love so much, hurts so very much. I know, however, each time I have been rejected, ridiculed, left out, lied about, ignored, etc., the cuts that these experiences create are just places for God to pour His grace into. He has done this time after time in the last three years. I am so grateful that God gave me a new understanding of how I could come to Him daily for His grace. It was just in time for my heart to be ripped out as I died to my family, to follow Christ. He has given me breath when it hurt so bad, I did not think I could even breathe. He has given me a place of safety in the arms and home of my faithful husband. He has become so much bigger to me, just when I needed Him the most.

Even down to old age, all my people shall prove
My sovereign, eternal, unchangeable love;
And then, when grey hair shall their temple adorn,
Like lambs shall they still in my bosom be borne.

What a loving and gentle shepherd Jesus is. I was lost, and now I am found. I was blind, and now I see. God is sovereign, eternal, and loves us perfectly. He does not leave us or forsake us, even when everything around us is screaming that we have been abandoned. We are not alone, when we put our trust in God and believe His word. The world will end, but His word will stand. The philosophies of this world, and all its vanity and dross will one day go away, but God's word will remain. He wins in the end. Satan is defeated, and even though he will try to deceive as many people as he can until Jesus returns, he has been defeated and all the authority in heaven and on earth are in Jesus Christ alone. No man has power in himself even to take the next breath, because in Christ all things exist and by Him all things consist.

The soul that on Jesus hath leaned for repose
I will not, I cannot, desert to his foes;
That soul, though all hell should endeavor to shake,
I'll never, no never, no never forsake.

CHAPTER 7

THE REALITY OF TODAY

Almost two and a half years have passed since God miraculously opened my eyes. He has been so good to me. My husband and I continued to take seminary classes and recently graduated. We have had several opportunities to speak about Mormonism. For years as a Mormon I stood up and "bore my testimony" as Mormons are encouraged to do during their fast and testimony meetings once a month. For years I bore testimony that the Mormon church was true, and that Joseph Smith was a true prophet. That false testimony was based on false information that I had been given by a deceptive organization. I now testify about what God has done for me. I testify that He alone can save, and that He is the only true and living God. I testify of His amazing grace and love. I testify that His word – the Bible is inerrant. I testify that He hears and answers our prayers. I testify that He will never leave us or forsake us, and that He will leave the ninety and nine and go after His lost sheep. I testify against false prophets and teachers.

The same week my husband and I graduated from seminary, my daughter was married in the Provo Temple. All my family was there, we were not. My heart broke for months leading up to the time that she covenanted all to the Mormon church. I tried to send her a card and letter, but it never made it to her. I have not had her address for well over a year. I had to send everything to her boyfriend's address, as he was trying to protect her from us. They see us as being antichrist, and of Satan. They have told us so. In this letter I mention my grandmother who passed away in 2002 who we called "Mema." She put her trust in Jesus Christ. She was never a Mormon. She never really knew what we believed as Mormons. We knew she loved us though. I believe if she had understood what we believed, she would have tried to teach us the truth. She heard us talk about Jesus; she did not realize however, it was not the Jesus of the Bible we were being taught to worship. This is the letter that I tried to send to my daughter. It sums up what is and has been in my heart:

I want you to know that marriage is pleasing to God. He said in Genesis 2: 24 "Therefore shall a man leave his father and his mother, and shall cleave unto his wife: and they shall be one flesh." God ordained marriage in the Garden of Eden.

You are about to become "one" in God's eyes.

*In order to be "one" there must be unity. Only the Spirit of God brings unity. Remember: as it says in **Galatians 5: 22 "But the fruit of the Spirit is love, joy, peace, longsuffering, kindness, goodness, faithfulness..."***

*If you both will submit your hearts and minds to our Almighty, Everlasting God by believing that Jesus paid it all for you, and trust Him every day with your lives, you will have unity in your marriage. You can rest in Him. He said in **Matthew 11: 28-29 "Come to Me, all you who labor and are heavy laden, and I will give you rest. Take my yoke upon you, and learn from Me; for I am gentle and lowly in heart: and you will find rest for your souls."***

124

There is someone else that is not with you today, other than me who loves you very much and would have loved to be with you during this time – Mema...

I want you to know that she has entered into her rest. She rested during her life too though by trusting in Jesus Christ. She is not in any temple or church today...she is with her Savior.

Someday if we all want to be together with her we must do what she did and trust in Christ alone.

He said Himself in **Matthew 12: 6 "...Yet in this place is One greater than the temple."** *He was referring to Himself.*

He also said in **John 2: 19 "...Destroy this temple, and in three days I will raise it up."** *Once again He was referring to His body – the temple.*

The day will come when the beautiful churches, temples, and cathedrals of this world will decay and crumble. Everything will pass away.

But one temple alone will remain forever – Jesus Christ our Almighty God.

As Peter said to the religious people of his day after having healed a lame man who laid helpless everyday by the gate of the temple ... **Acts 4: 10-12 "Let it be known to you all, and to all the people of Israel, that by the name of Jesus Christ of Nazareth, whom you crucified, whom God raised from the dead, by Him this man stands here before you whole. This is the stone which was rejected by you builders, which has become the chief cornerstone. Nor is there salvation in any other, for there is no other name under heaven given among men by which we must be saved."**

I know you look beautiful today. You have been beautiful since God created you years ago. With so many people there that I cherish and love...know this...

Days come and go, our lives take turns that we often do not understand, and one day our lives will all end...but there is One who goes on forever and is and has always been Eternal. It is my hope that the day will come that we all can be together, not in a building made with human hands, or outside among God's glorious creations of nature...but at the feet of Jesus Christ.

*And I say as it says in **1 Timothy 1: 17 "Now to the King eternal, immortal, invisible, to God who alone is wise, be honor and glory forever and ever. Amen."***

CHAPTER 8

MORMONISM: IN THEIR OWN WORDS

It states in the LDS publication entitled <u>Gospel</u> <u>Principles,</u> "Through the Prophet Joseph Smith, the Lord has expanded our understanding of some passages in the Bible. The Lord inspired the Prophet Joseph to restore truths to the Bible text that had been lost or changed since the original words were written." The Articles of Faith 1: 8, of the Mormon church states, "We believe the Bible to be the word of God as far as it is translated correctly."[63]

The Mormon church states about prophets the following:

1. We know that God communicated to the Church through His prophet.

2. A prophet is a man called by God to be His representative on earth.

3. When a prophet speaks for God, it is as if God were speaking.

4. A prophet teaches truth and interprets the word of God.

5. He receives revelations and directions from the Lord for our benefit.

6. He may see into the future and foretell coming events so that the world may be warned.

7. Modern prophets wear suits and carry briefcases.

8. A true prophet is always chosen by God and called through proper priesthood authority.

9. He has the right to revelation for the entire Church.

10. He holds "the keys of the kingdom", meaning that he has the authority to direct the entire Church and Kingdom of God on earth, including the administration of priesthood ordinances.

11. No person except the chosen Prophet and President can receive God's will for the entire membership of the Church.

12. We should follow his inspired teachings completely.

13. Whenever people choose to disregard, disobey, or distort any gospel principle or ordinance, whenever they reject the Lord's prophets, or whenever they fail to endure in faith, they distance themselves from God and begin to live in spiritual darkness.[64]

The following are statements that the Mormon Church makes about the priesthood:

1. The priesthood is the eternal power and authority of God.

2. Through the priesthood He created and governs the heavens and the earth. By this power the universe is kept in perfect order.

3. Through this power He accomplishes His work and glory, which is "to bring to pass the immortality and eternal life of man."

4. Our Heavenly Father delegates His priesthood power to worthy male members of the Church.

5. The priesthood enables them to act in God's name for the salvation of the human family. Through it they can be authorized to preach the gospel, administer the ordinances of salvation, and govern God's Kingdom on earth.

6. We must have priesthood authority to act in the name of God when performing the sacred ordinances of the gospel, such as baptism, confirmation, administration of the sacrament, and temple marriage.

7. If a man does not have the priesthood, even though he may be sincere, the Lord will not recognize ordinances he performs. These important ordinances must be performed on earth by men holding the priesthood.[65]

8. What is the priesthood? It is nothing more nor less than the power of God delegated to man by which man can act in the earth for the salvation of the human family, in the name of the Father and the Son and the Holy Ghost, and act legitimately; not assuming that authority, nor borrowing it from generations that are dead and gone, but authority that has been given in this day in which we live by ministering angels and spirits from above, direct from the presence of Almighty God...It is the same power and priesthood that was committed to the disciples of Christ while he was upon the

earth, that whatsoever they should bind on earth should be bound in heaven, and whatsoever they should lose on earth should be loosed in heaven.

9. What is priesthood? It is the government of God, whether on the earth or in the heavens, for if it is by that power, agency, or principle that all things are governed on the earth and in the heavens, and by that power that all things are upheld and sustained. It governs all things – and has to do with all things that God and truth are associated with. It is the power of God delegated to intelligences in the heavens and to men on the earth.[66]

The following are statements made about temples by the Church of Jesus Christ of Latter-day Saints:

1. The Atonement of Jesus Christ assures each of us that we will be resurrected and live forever. But if we are to live forever with our families in Heavenly Father's presence, we must do all that the Savior commands us to do. This includes being baptized and confirmed and receiving the ordinances of the temple.

2. Temples of the Church of Jesus Christ of Latter-day Saints are special buildings dedicated to the Lord. Worthy Church members may go there to receive sacred ordinances and make covenants with God. Like baptism, these ordinances and covenants are necessary for our salvation. They must be performed in the temples of the Lord. We also go to the temple to learn more about Heavenly Father and His Son, Jesus Christ. We gain a better understanding of our purpose in life and our relationship with Heavenly Father and Jesus Christ. We are taught about our pre-mortal existence, the meaning of earth life, and life after death.

3. All temple ordinances are performed by the power of the priesthood. Through this power, ordinances performed on earth are sealed, or bound, in heaven.

4. Only in the temple can we be sealed together as families. Marriage in the temple joins a man and woman as husband and wife eternally if they honor their covenants. Baptism and all other ordinances prepare us for this sacred event. When a man and woman are married in the temple, their children who are born thereafter also become part of their eternal family.[67]

5. God has commanded His people to build temples. In the temple we make sacred covenants and are endowed with, or are given, a gift of power and knowledge from on high. This power helps us in our daily lives and enables us to build God's Kingdom.

6. The Savior loves all people and desires their salvation. Yet millions of people have died without having any opportunity to hear the message of the restored gospel of Jesus Christ of receiving saving ordinances. Through His loving grace and mercy the Lord makes salvation possible for everyone who did not have the opportunity to receive, understand, and obey the gospel during their mortal lives. The gospel is preached to these deceased people in the spirit world. Members of the Church on earth perform the saving ordinances in behalf of their deceased ancestors and others. Deceased persons living in the spirit world would have the opportunity to accept or reject the gospel and the ordinances performed in their behalf.[68]

The following are statements about God (referred to as Heavenly Father in Mormonism) and the godhead by the Church of Jesus Christ of Latter-day Saints:

131

1. God the Eternal Father, whom we designate by the exalted name – title 'Elohim', is the literal Parent of our Lord and Savior Jesus Christ, and of the spirits of the human race.

2. I want to tell you, each and every one of you, that you are well acquainted with God our Heavenly Father, or the great Elohim. You are well acquainted with him, for there is not a soul of you but what has lived in his house and dwelt with him year after year; and yet you are seeking to become acquainted with him, when the fact is, you have merely forgotten what you did know. There is not a person here today but what is a son or a daughter of that Being. In the spirit world their spirits were first begotten and brought forth, and they lived there with their parents for ages before they came here.

3. God himself was once as we are now, and is an exalted man...If the veil were rent today...if you were to see him today, you would see him like a man in form – like yourselves in all the person, image, and very form as a man...it is the first principle of the Gospel to know for a certainty the Character of God, and to know that we may converse with him as one man converses with another, and that he was once a man like us; yea, that God himself, the Father of us all, dwelt on an earth, the same as Jesus Christ himself did; and I will show it from the Bible.

4. What did Jesus do? Why; I do the things I saw my Father do when worlds came rolling into existence. My Father worked out his kingdom with fear and trembling, and I must do the same; and when I get my kingdom, I shall present it to my Father, so that he may obtain kingdom upon kingdom, and it will exalt him in glory. He will then take his place, and thereby become exalted himself. So that Jesus treads in the tracks of his Father, and inherits what God did before; and

God is thus glorified and exalted in the salvation and exaltation of all his children.

5. The Father presides over the Godhead. Three glorified, exalted, and perfected personages comprise the Godhead or supreme presidency of the universe...They are: God the Father; God the Son; God the Holy Ghost...Though each God in the Godhead is a personage, separate and distinct from each of the others, yet they are 'one God'..., meaning that they are united as one in the attributes of perfection...Each occupies space and is and can be in but one place at one time, but each has power and influence that is everywhere present.

6. That Child to be born of Mary was begotten of Elohim, the Eternal Father, not in violation of natural law but in accordance with a higher manifestation thereof; and, the offspring from that association of supreme sanctity, celestial Sireship, and pure through mortal maternity, was of right to be called the 'Son of the Highest.'

7. Both the Father and the Son, being omnipotent Gods, are designated by the name-titles, Almighty, Almighty God, Lord Almighty, and Lord God Almighty. These designations signify that these holy beings have all power and unlimited might.

8. As far as man is concerned, all things center in Christ, He is the Firstborn of the Father. By obedience and devotion to the truth he attained that pinnacle of intelligence which ranked him as God, as the Lord Omnipotent, while yet in his pre-existent state. As such he became, under the Father, the Creator of this earth and of worlds without number; and he was then chosen to work out the infinite and eternal atonement, to come to this particular earth as the literal Son of the Father, and to put the whole plan of redemption, salvation, and exaltation in operation.

9. The Holy Ghost is the third member of the Godhead. He is a spirit, in the form of a man...The Holy Ghost is a personage of Spirit, and has a spirit body only. His mission is to bear witness of the Father and the Son and of all truth.

10. As a Spirit personage the Holy Ghost has size and dimensions. He does not fill the immensity of space, and cannot be everywhere present in person at the same time.

11. The Holy Ghost is the Messenger, or Comforter, which the Savior promised to send to his disciples after he was crucified. This comforter is, by his influence, to be a constant companion to every baptized person, and to administer unto the members of the Church by revelation and guidance, knowledge of the truth that they may walk in its light. It is the Holy Ghost who enlightens the mind of the truly baptized member.[69]

The following are doctrines and statements about covenants, law and grace from the Church of Jesus Christ of Latter-day Saints:

1. Within the Gospel, a covenant means a sacred agreement or mutual promise between God and a person or group of people. In making a covenant, God promises a blessing for obedience to particular commandments. He sets the terms of His covenants, and He reveals these terms to His prophets. If we choose to obey the terms of the covenant, we receive promised blessings. If we choose not to obey, He withholds the blessings, and in some instances a penalty also is given.

2. When we join the Church we make several covenants with God. We covenant with the Savior at baptism to take upon ourselves His name. He promises that 'as many as repent and are baptized in my name, which is Jesus Christ, and endure to the end, the same shall be saved (Doctrine and Covenants 18:

22). We covenant with the Lord as we partake of the sacrament. We promise to take His name upon ourselves, to remember Him, and to obey His commandments. We are promised that the Holy Spirit will be with us (Doctrine and Covenants 20: 77-79). When we receive temple ordinances, we make other sacred covenants and are promised exaltation for faithful obedience (Doctrine and Covenants 132).

3. The fullness of the gospel is called the new and everlasting covenant. It includes the covenants made at baptism, during the sacrament, in the temple, and at any other time. The Lord calls it everlasting because it is ordained by an everlasting God and because this covenant will never be changed...when we accept the new and everlasting covenant, we agree to repent, be baptized, receive the Holy Ghost, receive our endowments, receive the covenant of marriage in the temple, and follow and obey Christ to the end of our lives. As we keep our covenants, our Heavenly Father promises us that we will receive exaltation in the celestial kingdom.[70]

4. Covenants place us under a strong obligation to honor our commitments to God. To keep our covenants, we must give up activities or interests that prevent us from honoring those covenants.

5. Covenants are usually made by means of sacred ordinances, such as baptism. These ordinances are administered by priesthood authority. Through the ordinance of baptism, for example, we covenant to take upon ourselves the name of Jesus Christ, always remember Him, and keep His commandments. As we keep our part of the covenant, God promises the constant companionship of the Holy Ghost, a remission of our sins, and being born again.[71]

6. Grace: The enabling power from Jesus Christ that allows us to obtain blessings in this life and to gain eternal life and

exaltation after we have exercised faith, repented, and given our best effort to keep the commandments. Such divine help or strength is given through the mercy and love of Jesus Christ. We all need divine grace because of Adam's fall and also because of our weaknesses. Note: This is found in the Mormon missionary training manual as a definition of grace. Grace is not found in the other two Church publications which are referenced. Grace is not a concept spoken of much at all in Mormonism.[72]

The Mormon Church sees itself as the restored Church of Jesus Christ and Kingdom of God on the earth today. It considers itself the only true church on the earth today and holds itself out as having in its possession all the keys to death and hell. The following statements are statements about the Church:

1. On April 6, 1830, the Savior again directed the organizing of His Church on the earth (Doctrine and Covenants 20: 1). His Church is called The Church of Jesus Christ of Latter-day Saints (Doctrine and Covenants 115: 4). Christ is the head of His Church today, just as He was in ancient times. The Lord has said that it is "the only true and living church upon the face of the whole earth, with which I, the Lord, am well pleased" (Doctrine and Covenants 1: 30).

2. Since its restoration in 1830, The Church of Jesus Christ of Latter-day Saints has grown rapidly in membership. There are members in nearly every country in the world. The Church will continue to grow. As Christ said, 'This Gospel of the Kingdom shall be preached in all the world, for a witness unto all nations' (Joseph Smith – Matthew 1: 31). The Church will never again be taken from the earth. Its mission is to take the truth to every person. Thousands of years ago, the Lord said He would "set up a Kingdom, which shall never be

destroyed: and the Kingdom shall not be left to other people ...and it shall stand forever" (Daniel 2: 44).[73]

THE MORMON ARTICLES OF FAITH

1. We believe in God, the Eternal Father, and in His Son, Jesus Christ, and in the Holy Ghost.

2. We believe that men will be punished for their own sins, and not for Adam's transgression.

3. We believe that through the Atonement of Christ, all mankind may be saved, by obedience to the laws and ordinances of the Gospel.

4. We believe that the first principles and ordinances of the Gospel are: first, Faith in the Lord Jesus Christ; second, Repentance; third, Baptism by immersion for the remission of sins; fourth, Laying on of hands for the gift of the Holy Ghost.

5. We believe that a man must be called of God, by prophecy, and by the laying on of hands by those who are in authority, to preach the Gospel and administer in the ordinances thereof.

6. We believe in the same organization that existed in the Primitive Church, namely, apostles, prophets, pastors, teachers, evangelists, and so forth.

7. We believe in the gift of tongues, prophecy, revelation, visions, healing, interpretation of tongues, and so forth.

8. We believe the Bible to be the word of God as far as it is

translated correctly; we also believe the Book of Mormon to be the word of God.

ENDNOTES

1 Jerald and Sandra Tanner, Mormonism – Shadow or Reality (Utah
Lighthouse Ministry, 2008), p. 40.
2 Ibid. p. 49 – D.
3 Ibid. p. 32.
4 Ibid. p. 48-49.
5 Ibid. p. 203.
6 Ibid. p. 204.
7 Ibid. p. 143.
8 Ibid. p. 152.
9 Ibid. p. 42.
10 Ibid. p. 44.
11 Ibid. p. 46.
12 Ibid. p. 255.
13 Ibid. p. 213.
14 Ibid. p. 258-259.
15 Maria Anne Hirschmann, Hansi – The Girl Who Loved the
Swastika (Tyndale House Publishers, 1973).
16 Tanner, Mormonism, pp. 493-499.
17 Ibid., p. 490.
18 Ibid., pp. 486-492.
19 J. H. Beadle, Polygamy or the Mysteries and Crimes of
Mormonism(Library of Congress, 1882).
20 Ibid., p. i.
21 Ibid., p. 9.
22 Tanner, Mormonism, p. 203.
23 Ibid.
24 Ibid. p. 202.
25 The Doctrine and Covenants of the Church of Jesus Christ of
Latter-day Saints (The Church of Jesus Christ of Latter-day
Saints, 1981), pp. 266-273.
26 Ibid.
27 Fawn M. Brodie, No Man Knows My History – the Life of
Joseph Smith (Vintage Books, 1945), pp. 335-336.

28 *Tanner, Mormonism, p. 211.*
29 *Ibid., p. 213.*
30 *Ibid.*
31 *Ibid.*
32 *Ibid.*
33 *Ibid., p. 215.*
34 *Ibid., p. 219.*
35 *Ibid., p. 220.*
36 *Ibid., p. 221.*
37 *Ibid.*
38 *Ibid., p. 224.*
39 *Ibid., p. 230 – D.*
40 *Ibid., p. 230 – A.*
41 *Ibid., p. 209.*
42 *Ibid., p. 217.*
43 *Ibid.*
44 *Ibid.*
45 *Ibid., p. 205.*
46 *Ibid., p. 46.*
47 *Ibid., p. 47.*
48 *Ibid., p. 48-49.*
49 *Ibid., p. 36-37.*
50 *Ibid., p. 48.*
51 *Ibid., p. 49.*
52 *Ibid., p. 39.*
53 *Ibid., p. 47.*
54 *Ibid.*
55 *Ibid.*
56 *Ibid., p. 44.*
57 *Ibid.*
58 *Ibid., p. 43.*
59 *Ibid., p. 44.*
60 *Ibid., p. 43.*
61 *Ibid., p. 42.*
62 *Ibid., p. 44.*

63 The Church of Jesus Christ of Latter-day Saints, Gospel
Principles (Salt Lake City: The Church of Jesus Christ of Latter-
day Saints, 2009), 46.
64 Gospel Principles 39-42.
65 The Church of Jesus Christ of Latter-day Saints, Preach My
Gospel (Salt Lake City: The Church of Jesus Christ of Latter-day
Saints, 2004), 33.
66 Gospel Principles 67.
67 The Church of Jesus Christ of Latter-day Saints, Doctrines of
the Gospel(Salt Lake City: The Church of Jesus Christ of Latter-
day Saints, 2004) 67-68.
68 Gospel Principles 233-235.
69 Preach My Gospel 86.
70 Doctrines of the Gospel 6-12.
71 Gospel Principles 81-84.
72 Preach My Gospel 70.
73 Gospel Principles 97-100.
74 The Church of Jesus Christ of Latter-day Saints, The Articles
of Faith(Salt Lake City: The Church of Jesus Christ of Latter-day
Saints, 1981) 60-61.

ABOUT THE AUTHOR

Shawna K. Lindsey was a Mormon from 1979 until 2009. While not attending the Mormon Church in 1983, she was witnessed to by a relative and became a born again believer in Jesus Christ. Not knowing enough about the Bible, she went back to the Mormon Church in 1984 as a brand new Christian. She was married in the Salt Lake City Temple in 1984 and did Mormon temple work in many temples over the next 23 years. God miraculously opened her eyes to the truth of Mormonism on Easter Sunday 2009, after a year of intensive instruction and study of the New Testament. She now speaks publicly about the hidden doctrines of Mormonism, its little known seditious history, and it's similarity to Islam. She has a law degree and has recently earned a Doctorate in Theology.

www.ingramcontent.com/pod-product-compliance
Lightning Source LLC
Chambersburg PA
CBHW061727020426
42331CB00006B/1125